Finding
Fulfillment:

Wisdom for Practical Living

Finding Fulfillment:

Wisdom for Practical Living

by
Paul Serwinek, Ph.D.

Library of Congress Catalog Card No. 96-61254

ISBN 1-56550-048-2

Printed in the United States of America

Cover art :Maxine Vertz
Cover graphics and design: Robert Brekke

Vision Books International
3360 Coffey Lane
Santa Rosa, CA 95403
707-542-1440 800-377-3431
FAX 707-542-1004

Dedicated to Marlene, Matt,
Alissa and Katie, my family, who
provided the inspiration for this volume

TABLE OF CONTENTS

Preface   **vii**

Chapter 1
Fate or Faith?   1

Chapter 2
Problems and Positives   12

Chapter 3
Goal-Growing   28

Chapter 4
Body Basics (Fitness)   47

Chapter 5
Acquiring Allegiance (Faith)   64

Chapter 6
Living Legacy (Family)   83

Chapter 7
Abundant Affluence (Fortune)   105

Chapter 8
Nurturing Networks (Friends)   124

Chapter 9
Creative Careers (Finance)   142

Chapter 10
Essential Education (Faculties)   160

Chapter 11
Dominant Dreams (Fame)   180

Chapter 12
The Secret of Balance   197

Chapter 13
A New Beginning   217

PREFACE

I was twenty-two years old, married not quite a year, and had a job that I thought would provide well for my wife and me with potential for advancement. My wife, Marlene, was pregnant with our first child, and I felt life couldn't get any better. But suddenly, the newspaper I was working for went on strike. Whispered comments from those "on high" came to me that we'd better look for other work as this strike threatened to be a long one. What was I to do? I had no college degree, I didn't have a wealthy family. I was confused, disillusioned and frankly, I was scared. My father was a simple man who had worked as a machinist in a tool shop, and though I loved and admired him greatly, I couldn't picture myself going the route he had taken. Whom could I turn to for advice? Who could help me make a career decision at this critical time in my life?

I think we've all been there and wished there were a wise and trusted friend we could go to for advice. "If only there was someone who has gone through experiences similar to those I am going through now, someone to offer me guidance from their experience! Someone who could say, 'This is what really worked for me.' " We all can use a mentor for personal growth. I believe this book can help the reader develop insights, not just on career success, but also on what is more important: life success—soul success.

The practical wisdom I've received over the years I have gleaned from many sources, including my own experience. I'm always amazed that the most profound advice and life outlook is always in harmony with the wisdom of ages. So if you are at a point in life where you are reassessing your outlook and options, if you find yourself preparing or planning for the next stage of your life, you'll find what you need here. Whether you are a young adult contemplating your options with respect to raising a family or your initial career move, or whether you are a seasoned parent deciding on a new primary focus now that your children are on their own, or you're an adult in mid-life just realizing you've lost the excitement life once had for you and you desperately want it back, there is hope! I can offer you the aid of time-tested principles of living, not the ever-changing fads of social and psychological commentators. All the practical application I offer is completely compatible with the ideas for living given in the most respected guide for living ever available, the Bible. I offer you a source for ideas and practical suggestions you can use immediately and experience immediate results that will transform your life.

Are you at a crossroads in your life? It's decision-making time, but you're just not sure of your next move. Or maybe something's just missing, you're not sure what. You just aren't satisfied with life as it is. Whether you are reassessing your life, preparing for the next important step, or searching for that missing piece, there are some timeless principles worth exploring before you make your next move.

The "standards" in our society change so rapidly that there appears to be no standard at all. Many people with whom I speak wonder whether the advice they grew up with or the truths in our biblical heritage can be applied to life in this age.

I came up against it in the late sixties and early seventies when Marlene and I were raising our children, Matt, Alissa, and Katie. Child psychologists had begun claiming that children should be encouraged to explore and discover for themselves which lifestyle worked for them. It was said that parents shouldn't burden children with preconceived ideas of right or wrong. Children should be free to form their own moralities. This unrestrictive environment would foster intellectual growth and social competence, claimed the theorists.

This thinking, though, was in direct opposition to the age-old wisdom of our Western heritage. The Bible, for example, states, "Train up a child in the way he should go, and when he is old he will not turn from it." (Proverbs 22:6) And further, "These commandments that I give you...impress them on your children. Talk about them when you sit at home and when you walk along the road, when you lie down and when you get up." (Deuteronomy 6:6,7)

What were we to believe as young parents? Should we follow traditional wisdom or the latest, "most advanced" ideas in child development? It's true, we admitted; science had transformed the world for the better with continuing medical discoveries and new labor-saving electronic devices. Was this also going to be true with the latest so-called scientific, psychological, and social discoveries? We had to decide. We knew we had only one chance to raise our children. Which of the two divergent paths should we take? We chose the wisdom of the ages.

Within a few years the results of these social theories began to be published. Evidence concluded that for optimum development children need the security of guidelines for living. They need the advantage of parental experience rather than the latitude to learn their social skills by trial and error. How grateful we were we had made the correct choice! How grateful we were to have chosen the Bible's time-proven guidelines for parenting! To this day, Marlene and I look at Matt, Alissa, and Katie, who are now young adults of whom we are so proud, and give thanks that we had the practical, biblical guidance we did.

We've found that the wisdom of the Bible brought success to every area of life to which we applied it. The purpose of this book is to encourage others also to have success in their lives in all areas by exploring biblical truth and practical principles for living. All the ideas presented are in harmony with scripture. I am writing to Christians who already value biblical truth and also to those who may not be Christians, but who have minds open to truth that works.

Many Christians inadvertently inhibit the joy of life (one of the fruits of God's spirit listed in Galatians 5:22) by focusing only on the future joy of being with Christ and missing out on the joy of living promised now. This is a call to you to "let your light shine" (Matthew 6:23) as Scripture encourages. I hope this book encourages you to use this philosophy of living for a more meaningful and fulfilling life, one you can take pride in and become a "shining" example of the power of God's Word to those who don't yet know Him. The Bible exhorts, "Be not afraid, O land; be glad and rejoice." (Joel 2:21) A Christian should not miss out on the joy of living.

If you are not a Christian, the principles in this book can still work for you. First, the beauty of the Christian-living philosophy is that you don't have to be a believer to gain its benefits. "He causes His sun to rise upon the evil and the good." You merely have to live by His precepts to benefit from them. History and current scientific research have verified the exceptional wisdom contained in the pages of the Bible. Incorporate them into your life and see for yourself. You don't have to live by all of them at once. Each principle, or Transformation as I call them, as you choose to apply it, will bring its own reward. To the extent you apply them, your life will be blessed. Ultimately, it is my hope that as you use His precepts for living, you'll come to know the One from whom they flow.

There is a very interesting phenomenon at work in our society. As we become more technologically innovative, and as life becomes more complex with myriad options, there is a simultaneous desire to get back to some basics that will simplify life. The further our society advances in science and in technology to the point where our physical way of life is so far removed from that of our parents and even so vastly different from twenty years ago, the more the elements of success in living remain the same! All the discoveries in psychology and sociology, rather than leading us further from our ancestors' way of life, tend to confirm the ancient wisdom. In one respect, physically, we're further removed from our heritage, but in another, which constitutes the most productive way of living, we keep coming back to the time-tested principles of the past. In fact, every breakthrough in psychology that, on first impression, appears to be a monumental discovery, upon further consideration just confirms the soundness of the wisdom of the past.

What I've done is enumerate some of the most powerful principles of living, principles I've discerned from my thirty years of study, research, and living. I've then shown by references in the Bible that these are the same ideas that have stood the test of time but only have been updated and stated in the vernacular of our age. The truths are no different, just as potent as ever. The same ideas, if followed, that led to fulfillment and joy then will lead to the same treasure today. Conversely, any theories that contradict the truths of biblical origin are invariably exposed to be erroneous when the results of living by them are studied over the long term.

Unfortunately, more than a few Christians I've met have the erroneous idea that they must constantly suffer in this life. Nothing can be further from the truth. The Bible says, "God, who richly provides us with everything for our enjoyment..." (1 Timothy 6:17) This is talking about now, not some future life. Yes, we do suffer pain and loss at times. But our lives as a whole can be joyful; this is a promise from God. Accept it and believe it! Your life can and will be filled with enjoyment if you merely follow the principles He outlined ages ago.

Advice is cheap, of course. Often I hear of psychologists purporting to lead others while their own lives are in shambles. There are family counselors guiding others, though they themselves have never had an enduring relationship with a spouse or partner or children of whom they could be proud. I know a number of sales motivational speakers who themselves could not succeed in a sales career but somehow feel qualified to offer advice about sales to others in sales seminars. They call themselves "sales experts."

How is the advice here different? Everything I suggest here I have personally tested and used with practical, successful results. When I tell you about goal attainment, I personally have employed the techniques mentioned with astounding results. I didn't start on a successful path until I was thirty years old. Coming from a blue-collar background, it took me years to realize the wisdom of pursuing a college education, but once I did I earned a bachelor's degree, a master's degree in business administration, and a doctorate in social psychology. I also built a successful small business that has provided wealth and security for my family, all the while making substantial progress in other facets of life. When I tell you about family relationships, I can point to a happy, enduring marriage to Marlene and three well-adjusted children. When I tell you about physical fitness, I can submit my personal program of exercise that I have maintained for many years. In all the major areas of life in which I offer suggestions, I can document exceptional results either from personal experience or from the experiences of ordinary people. Finally, I can assure you every bit of this advice is in harmony with the wisdom found in the Bible. That's why it has worked for me and why it will work for you.

My goal in writing this book is that as you read it and work with it, your life will be transformed for the better. Over the years, I've discovered some amazing principles of living that, when followed, are life-transforming. In each section I have highlighted these principles as "Transformations." By living these principles, your life will be transformed. Some of these Transformations are accompanied by scriptural references to verify they are directly based upon biblical truths. On my journey through life, I made an intriguing discovery. Every successful breakthrough in modern social science that has been shown to be functional is invariably in harmony with Scripture. On the other hand, each so-called discovery that is in opposition to Scripture has, in time, been proven by further research by social scientists themselves to be unfounded. That in itself has strengthened my faith.

A good example of this is the way psychologists have treated the writings of Sigmund Freud over the years. His theories at one time were considered the course of wisdom in psychology. Though his novel ideas were quite pessimistic about human nature, they were a stark contrast from the scriptural idea that man "was created in the image of God." The majority of psychologists and psychiatrists accepted his views. Fortunately, as more research was done and more of his ideas were put to the test, scientists began to realize he imputed the dysfunction of severely emotionally scarred patients to all humans. Over time, the scriptural perspective has been vindicated. Psychologists now esteem him for his innovation but recognize that his extreme pessimism need not be accepted. No doubt many were helped by his research, but how many others were hindered from attaining proper emotional healing following his extreme perspective? Those heeding the unchanging principles of Scripture were not so affected.

My guidelines for living do not presuppose any biblical training or faith, for that matter. These reality principles will work for you regardless of your personal beliefs. Scriptural principles are free to be employed by anyone, regardless of personal faith. I also write without continuous reference to the spiritual because I feel these principles can help you right now, no matter where you are in life's journey and no matter what your level of faith in a Higher Power.

The wonderful thing about these transcending life principles is that they can be employed one by one without a full understanding of how or why they work and even without, for a time, realizing your indebtedness to a Higher Power. As a Christian, I realize this is an example of the kindness and mercy of God, who offers his benevolence to all; as Scripture says, "He causes his sun to rise on the evil and the good." (Matthew 5:45) You'll also be able to share these ideas with friends and family, those who have come to recognize their need for commitment to a power greater than themselves. For example, you'll notice that Chapter 5, the section about faith, is purposely written for someone with little or no understanding of what spirituality really is. I present evidence that your need for communion with a power greater than yourself is a necessary aspect of life.

Each chapter also contains a response section. I have suggested an assignment or activity for you to act on. In most cases, they are simple mental exercises which help you learn by doing and in the process, discover something valuable about yourself. Self-disclosure is an important ability we all need.

Another feature is the inclusion of scriptural quotations after many of the transformational thoughts highlighted. These are included to verify that the ideas presented as powerful principles of living are a confirmation of the wisdom that has remained relevant through the ages. I have not placed scriptural references by all the Transformation points, only by the major ones and by those that may appear at first glance to be less obvious allusions to scriptural tenets.

Finally, my intentions here are three-fold. Over the years, I've searched for and found (sometimes stumbled upon might be more accurate) basic principles for living that have given me the direction and guidance I needed. I share them with you.

Second, I emphasize that these living rules are fully in harmony with Christian principles. I've heard so-called authorities promote what they consider new discoveries for modern living, and at the same time denigrate Christian heritage, never realizing that their so-called discoveries were stated more succinctly and clearly in the pages of the Bible. The most useful ideas in modern psychology, sociology, and mental and emotional health are all compatible with Christianity and have often served as inadvertent allusions to biblical tenets written long ago. A person living by biblical principles is not overlooking modern research. He or she is living proof of the success of these principles.

My third point is that we are not destined to constant suffering in this life. Of course there will be problems, but we do not have to make a choice between living as a suffering Christian and giving up our faith in order to enjoy life now. The Bible says, "Blessed are all who fear the Lord, who walk in his ways. You will eat the fruit of your labor; blessings and prosperity will be yours." (Psalm 128:1,2) That can't be much clearer. God intends life to be joyful!

My appeal is in harmony with the challenge set out in Scripture, "Put me to the proof, says the Lord of Hosts, and see if I do not open windows in the sky and pour a blessing on you as there is need." (Malachi 3:10) These words are applicable to Christians or non-Christians. Incorporate these living principles, these Transformations, into your life and enjoy the marvelous changes that will come.

CHAPTER 1

Fate or Faith?

Do you look forward to a life of continual suffering? I sure don't! But some people mistakenly believe that's what Christianity is. Nothing could be further from the truth! The wisdom of the ages is of immense value "holding promise for both the present life and the life to come." (1 Timothy 4:8) As a Christian you can expect aid in making your present life a life filled with enjoyment. (1 Timothy 6:17) And if you are not a Christian, you can still apply the timeless wisdom of the ages to make your life vibrant and exciting. The Bible offers the guidance and practical wisdom need-ed for living now. To the extent you live by this practical advice, you will be spared unnecessary difficulties. Take note of the assessment of this Divine Wisdom described in Psalm 19:7,8,11:

> The law of the LORD is perfect, reviving the soul.

> The statutes of the LORD are trustworthy, making wise the simple.

> The precepts of the LORD are right, giving joy to the heart.

> The commands of the LORD are radiant, giving light to the eyes.

> By them is your servant warned; in keeping them there is great reward.

You may not have realized that the wisdom of the ages and, specifically, the wisdom of the Bible is inherently optimistic. I have friends who come from families plagued with alcoholism, for example. Whenever they thought conditions were finally going to improve, their fathers would lapse into another drunken binge, lose jobs, and the cycle of suffering would begin all over again. It is difficult to maintain an optimistic outlook given such experi-ences. For me, though, optimism has been more easily main-tained. Though coming from a blue-collar background, I observed that my father could always find another job when he lost one due to economic conditions. He was willing to take any kind of work to provide for his family. We always had the necessities—no matter how bleak circumstances appeared on a particular day.

I've learned that whenever I begin to develop a negative outlook or go through a period of depression, I can say to myself, "I know I'm just tired now. Wait till tomorrow when I'm feeling better or fully awake. I'll see things more clearly then."

I ask you to do the same, suspend judgment about any of the assertions I make, and concede you may have picked up a negative outlook along the way. Suspend judgment and give the wisdom of the ages a chance to work in your life!

No Regrets

Stop and think for a moment: If you could do it all over again, how much of your life would you change? How much of your past would you alter? How many of your past experiences would you rather forego to eliminate the difficulties, the pain, the sorrow, the embarrassment, and the malaise of unhappiness? Looking back, how many missed opportunities do you wish you could encounter again to take advantage of them? What past relationships might have been worth pursuing? What choices could you have made differently?

I asked these questions of myself not too many years ago and was startled to realize that there was very little I would change. Even if I were granted the proverbial three wishes by providence, I'd prefer to leave my past unaltered. What a surprising revelation! What may be more surprising, when you finish this book you may feel the same way! When you realize, and you will, that your present life status can always be changed by current actions, you will see no need to be so concerned with the past. Why worry about reliving the past when you can begin a transformation to become the person you've dreamed of being from the present moment forward?

You can transform your life into the life you've dreamed of. I've diligently studied the field of self-development for some thirty years now. I've researched and experimented in my own life. I've tried many ideas that have failed miserably, but I've also tried others that have been wonderfully successful. The principles you need to insure that your life, from the present moment, is one of fulfillment and bliss are easy to understand and act upon. The one critical factor is this: I knew if I had present dreams, I could attain them in the future, but I was happy with the progress I had made to this point. If you are not content with your present life, you can come to that point. You'll be satisfied with where you are now and have no desire to redo or regret your past.

When I recognized that I was content and happy, I analyzed how I had come to that point. What had I done or not done to arrive at what I considered an enviable position? After considerable thought, I realized there were several important principles I had learned to apply. Then I realized these ideas were universal and could be communicated. I had discovered some keys to a life of contentment and joy which I could pass on.

If you are searching for answers to improve your life, you are in an enviable position yourself. How often do people come to the point where they consciously admit they want something better for themselves? The fact that you are reading this is an indication that you have reached the point of wanting something better for yourself and have begun to do something about it. That is the first and most important step! How many people do you know who believed that circumstances could never change for them? They are destined to live a life far below what it could be. By your actions, you have already pressed beyond the majority!

Is it Fate?

In the Gilbert and Sullivan operetta, *The Pirates of Penzance*, the hero was a young man who, due to fate, had been raised on a ship at sea and had never ventured on dry land until he was an adult. The comic story goes that he had never seen a woman except the not-so-fair maiden who was a fellow shipmate. He always believed what he had been told by her, that she was the prettiest, fairest maiden a man could ever desire. Only when he was allowed to venture from the ship for the first time did he realize that he had been deceived. He met other women who were beautiful, and his eyes were opened. Now his horizons expanded. Now he had choices. He was overjoyed to find his romantic life could be far more appealing.

Many people live life that way, believing in fate, limiting their options. They assume that fate has dealt them a hand, and they have no choices and few opportunities. As a result they never dare venture further, never seek something better. They are like the pirate who was confined to the ship, thinking he had no options. Their tragedy is confinement that is self-imposed! Can you see how privileged you are to be where you are in life at this moment? The fact that you picked up this book proves you do not fully believe the myth of fate. You believe something better is possible, and you're doing something about it.

If you have a desire for a better life, you can have it, though you may not even know at the moment what that better life could be. The critical point is that by wanting something better—and believing—it's possible. You would not have picked up this book unless deep down you thought a better life was possible. Statistically, you have already set yourself apart from the 95 percent of the people around you who lack the ambition to make the effort to specifically work on improving their lives.

If you believe transformation of your life for the better is possible, why would you be concerned with changing the past, revising the past, worrying about the past? You can start living the present to attain whatever was missing from the past. It's much more functional to say, "I'm content with my present life and I've let the past go." At the moment you may not be ready to make the big commitment to letting the past go and accepting the present. But be open to the dynamic principles of living, and you'll naturally want to try them out. As each Transformation improves your life, you'll be willing to rid yourself of the past. Whether it was the sorrow of the past or the beautiful memories of a past that you are certain can never be enjoyed again, both can limit your current joy. Use the past as a motivator, rather than a roadblock, to the present.

Let's look at your life as unknown territory. You are fighting your way through a wilderness, knowing nothing about what signs to look for or even where you really plan to end up. Then you meet a wilderness guide. He helps you decide what your destination is and teaches you the principles of reading the signs along the way to take the right path to get there. No two lives are the same. But the principles of reading the signs along the way are. Your life isn't like mine. But we all face disappointments and must deal with our own mortality. The life principles here can help you to learn how to read the signs and map out your path.

I wasn't always so contented. When I was in my twenties, I had a successful marriage, a job that provided for my family, but I had just lost the joy and excitement I had once had. The sparkle was gone. Something was missing from my life. A dullness, a lack of vitality, permeated my days. I couldn't put my finger on it, but something was definitely lacking. Since then, I have had others describe to me similar feelings. I didn't know if I had lost something along the way or if there were some quality I had never had to begin with. All I knew was that I was desperate to recover or to discover it. Thus began my search, some thirty years ago, for the "secrets" that would bring me true happiness. During this period, I worked first to discover these secrets, then to implement them and then to perfect their use. Over the years of this journey, I have been open to suggestions and ideas from others and have tried them and continued them when they worked. These aren't secrets after all, but they are powerful, time-tested principles which I've compiled.

Studies have shown that one of the surest ways to succeed in a corporate career is to attach yourself to an associate in the company who is already successful. By following her example or by following his advice, you are led step-by-step in first founding and then building your career. This person becomes your mentor. She is able to relate what she has done to make it to the enviable position of authority she possesses. You have confidence in her advice since you recognize her ideas are not merely theoretical but are practical suggestions that really work. You know that if you follow the path she outlines for you, you have an excellent chance for success. Your own success becomes more of a probability than a possibility. It worked for her, and there is every reason to believe it will work for you. Why not accept the wisdom of experience?

Fortunately, I learned early not to follow the advice of just anyone calling himself "expert." I sought advice from those who demonstrated that they had obtained what they promised, following exactly the steps they suggested. I also sought the principles of living that have endured. The assertion is made in the Bible that "All scripture is God-breathed and is useful for teaching, rebuking, correcting and training." (2 Timothy 3:16) My research has proved this to be undeniably true. I've spent over thirty years researching, compiling, and applying such advice. Some of the successful practices I learned from others worked immediately; some advice was sound but didn't work until modified to be more practical, and some I learned from trial and error. Every principle you read here, I have applied in my life with good results. What you won't see here are all the ideas I tried which sounded reasonable but proved to be dismal failures. I have divided the practical from the theoretical, the best from the better, the principles I can truly say work, since I can testify that they worked in my life.

Life Facets

I discovered that our lives can be divided into eight areas, or arenas. If we ask ourselves how we are doing in each of these roles and take the steps necessary to bring our lives into harmony with our expectations in each of these, the inevitable results are we find ourselves contented and satisfied. You might look at it as a puzzle with eight pieces. Once you recognize the eight pieces, find what those pieces mean to you, and then put them together in a way that fits for you, a harmonious picture emerges. Each piece by itself can provide a measure of joy and satisfaction, but only when all eight are accounted for and placed in order, does the picture of your life come into focus. When this happens, the enjoyment and satisfaction in life surpasses all expectations.

I've developed the acronym, "BALANCED," to make these areas easy to remember. On a regular basis, I run through this checklist of eight aspects of life mentally to be certain I have the eight puzzle pieces in proper perspective or focus for me. These are the eight essential roles of life that must be acknowledged and then brought into harmony with your personal picture:

> BODY (Fitness)
>
> ALLEGIANCE (Faith)
>
> LEGACY (Family)
>
> AFFLUENCE (Fortune)
>
> NETWORK (Friends)
>
> CAREER (Finances)
>
> EDUCATION (Faculties)
>
> DREAMS (Fame)

Here they are in a little more detail:

(1) BODY—personal health care that provides the energy for growth in all aspects of life.

(2) ALLEGIANCE—the importance of finding meaning in life and attaining a spiritual outlook regardless of religious affiliation.

(3) LEGACY—successful living with your spouse, children, and parents.

(4) AFFLUENCE—wealth and how to provide the financing for all of life's activities.

(5) NETWORKS—building and maintaining friendships.

(6) CAREER—occupational choices and job advancement.

(7) EDUCATION—perfecting one's mental and emotional capabilities; an on-going program for personal growth.

(8) DREAMS—pursuit of an avocation either in conjunction with or in addition to one's financial career; hobbies and enjoyable activities to fill one's life.

I know it sounds simple. But I found that by picturing what I wanted in these eight dimensions, then taking the necessary steps to bring my life into harmony with them, I enjoyed the surge of confidence and contentment. I realized for the first time, I had harmony in my life. The recipe is simple to explain. Working it out will take some effort, but it's worth it.

The revelation of your personal confidence and worth, when it comes to you, is a momentous occasion! You will feel about yourself as the Bible already says about you, that you are "the image and glory of God." (1 Corinthians 11:7) Now it's your turn: Examine each of your life roles one at a time; then put them in the order that is right for you.

You will find when you run through this checklist that you may already be satisfied with the results in certain life facets—even in your present circumstances. For example, you may already be contented with how your career is going or with the network of friends you now have. If so, you are already that much closer to your goal of a fulfilling life. You need only identify the areas that need more work in your life and considering each, one at a time, follow the suggestions in this book which work for you.

The chapters have been arranged to include each of the life arenas and each of the important life skills you must master. These skills, like goal setting or problem-solving, can be used to bring into focus your vision for each of life's aspects. Throughout the book you will find important principles highlighted that must be understood and incorporated into your personal life. Look for these principles. Here are examples of several important ones that you'll understand and master:

(1) Knowing yourself—recognizing what is important to you and fulfilling those desires.

(2) Maintaining a proper balance in all areas of life—not neglecting any aspect of the eight facets of life.

(3) Working toward incorporating your avocation into your vocation with the ultimate goal of merging these two into one.

(4) Realizing that you deserve to enjoy the inheritance of the world around you.

In each life facet, you will isolate several key principles that must be understood and practiced for success in that area. Since these principles have to do with the way you think and perceive, I call them Transformations because they may require a new way of thinking. I've come to understand that many of my past problems and the problems of those with whom I work are directly attributable to a faulty thinking pattern. When I've recognized my error and transformed my thinking to a more realistic and practical pattern, problems vanished.

Here's a simple example. A popular way of dealing with physical pain in our culture is to eliminate pain with little thought to the underlying cause of the pain. A simple but important Transformation in thinking I learned is that physical pain has a positive aspect to it. Physical pain is my body's way of telling me a change in the way I treat my body is necessary. When I realized this for the first time, I stopped complaining that I had headaches in the late morning and started to ask, "What is my body trying to tell me?" I learned that my problem was a matter of low blood sugar that was easily corrected. The simple Transformation of recognizing that pain has a value eliminated many other potential health problems. That change in perception helped me to circumvent years of agony. Grasping any one such Transformation and putting it into practice will immediately change your life for the better.

Each chapter will isolate several such mental Transformations that you might consider adopting. Really, so much of life is merely a matter of outlook. Adjusting your outlook, transforming the way you perceive a habitual daily practice will almost magically alleviate many negatives in your life. As I mentioned, a feature of these discussions is that each major Transformation idea is isolated with a biblical reference where the link to Scripture may not appear clear. This will provide support that these principles are not new, they are just reworded for modern use. As stated in the Preface, current research in the social sciences confirms the scriptural sages. In each life area (Career, Friendship, Financial Security, etc.) a few simple adjustments in your viewpoint will yield tremendous results. So specifically look for the Transformation that will be highlighted. Meditate on it, and redesign your thinking accordingly.

TRANSFORMATION:

A voluntary change of perception will immediately eliminate many of life's problems.

"To be made new in the attitude of your minds; and to put on the new self." (Ephesians 4:23,24)

Have you heard some of these ideas before? Yes. Are they elementary ideas? Yes. However, we'll work on simple techniques to help implement these into all facets of life. What's more, though, there are countless techniques for attaining proficiency in the eight life facets. I will identify those techniques that are most powerful and most easily implemented. This is not to say other ideas would not work, but only that the ones presented here are the ones most easily understood and put into practice. Why complicate things?

The quest is an enjoyable journey, one to anticipate with excitement. It's like climbing a difficult, circuitous trail up the side of a mountain and, reaching the peak, being rewarded with a spectacular view. The effort and inconvenience were worth the price in exchange for the beauty and joy of the moment. Your life can be better than it is. You can and will find the contentment you are craving. That's what God wants for you! Each chapter will assist you in dealing with some of the problems you are certain to encounter in living.

Mankind has been struggling with life's aspects for countless generations. Yet the principles of true happiness are not secrets; they have been known and practiced for far longer than we may realize. These ideas have stood the test of time and are still relevant today.

> *"Yesterday is a dream and tomorrow a vision, only this day is a reality. If I live this day well, yesterday becomes a dream of happiness and tomorrow becomes a vision of hope."*
> *(Sanskrit Proverb Circa 2500 BC)*

As an additional motivation, remember the words of the greatest teacher of all times, Jesus: "Ask and it will be given to you; seek and you will find; knock and the door will be opened to you." (Matthew 7:7)

CHAPTER 2

Problems and Positives

Unexpected and seemingly insurmountable problems are facts of life. I'll never forget the feeling of panic that seized me the moment I was called into the owner's office and fired from my position as an insurance agency representative. It took every ounce of self-control to force my body to literally stop from shaking. I was in my thirties at the time and had just purchased a new home and a new car. I had three young children, yet in one moment all my resources seemed to evaporate before me. I still vividly recall thinking "Why is this happening to me? What am I going to do?" as I drove home in a daze.

Fortunately, I tempered my initial reaction of panic and withheld thoughts of ruin for several hours till I could gain control of my emotions. I prayed for guidance. Within a couple of hours, though still numb with fear, I mustered up enough faith to believe there must be a way out and that I would find it. Remarkably, once I made this resolve, ideas and plans started to pop into my head. The next day I would prepare a letter to all my clients promising them that I would continue to serve their needs. I'd rent office space and contact companies one by one to line up the products I'd need to continue.

Each time I'd begin to sense that negative feeling of fear creeping back, I'd tell myself, "I know I'm just exhausted right now, and I'm not going to dwell on this fear!"

Now I look back on that original problem as a positive milestone in my life. If I hadn't been forced to struggle with adversity then, I might never have started a profitable small business that has provided opportunities for personal growth and substantial remuneration over the years. Usually, problems are opportunities in disguise.

Many a theologian and philosopher have struggled with the problem of why there are problems. In other words, why, if there is a God, does he allow suffering and difficulties that afflict believers in particular? Wouldn't God want to spare those faithful to him? This universal lament is covered in a later chapter. In the meantime, if God were to absolve his children from suffering, the motive for serving Him would always be questioned. Was it for purely selfish motives or out of love for God? No, God does not shelter believers from difficulties, but there is a major concession given. God does promise Christians help through difficulties and the assistance comes in unexpected ways. One of the these is the encouragement given in Scripture to believers weathering problems to "persevere in prayer." (Romans 12:12) The promise is also given at Isaiah 40:31, "...but those who hope in the Lord will renew their strength. They will soar on wings like eagles; they will run and not grow weary, they will walk and not be faint."

The admonition on living given in Scripture helps us avoid immeasurable problems in the first place. For example, the advice on avoiding excesses in food and drink, if followed, spares us from any number of health problems. However, the proper outlook toward problems is the most immediate support offered. Problems are short-term, while joy and happiness are enduring. The Lord also promises us in 2 Timothy 1:7, "For God did not give us a spirit of timidity, but a spirit of power."

There will be problems, but please don't expect that life must be a series of one emergency after another, one adversity after another. We have reason to be joyful. Philippians 4:4 emphasizes the point, "Rejoice in the Lord always, I will say it again: Rejoice." When you understand and internalize the proper perspective toward problems, you'll be amazed at how they lose their original magnitude. Let's work on this outlook and on some practical advice for resolving difficulties when they arise.

It's Now

At times I need to remind myself that this moment is reality. Life is now, not some future event. Now is the time to be living, to be alive. Unfortunately, many people fritter life away by spending today daydreaming about tomorrow. That's not living. That's simply one mechanism for avoiding problems and putting up with a life of unhappiness, but that's not for you. Granted, continued daydreaming enables you to circumvent some problems that would arise if you were living in reality. But, look at the progression: Daydreaming, though essential, may continue until someone feels it's too late to act and then resigns himself to a passive life. It becomes easy then to rationalize, "It wasn't meant to be. It's foolish to make a move now at this late date. I'll be content with the measure of security I have." That is what I call "mind-living," while the day-to-day habitual roles our bodies act out can be purely "physical living." Neither is the goal we seek in "total-living."

The reasons for this tragedy of life slipping away are simply understood. First of all, it's much easier to follow the course of least resistance. You can float along in the direction the currents of life take you with little effort. You don't have to do much navigating, simply steering around a few obstacles here and there or staying clear of uncomfortable events will get you by. Really, though, this strategy allows the currents (events) of life to choose for you. This hesitance to act also occurs because you value security, a very basic need for all living things. Rather than venturing out into the deep unknown and open sea, you can choose to stay close to the shoreline. This provides protection from unforeseen events and assures you of a safe harbor if needed. But alas, remember this journey of your life here is limited. You don't have the luxury of unlimited time to live as though the journey can be taken haphazardly. Second chances don't always come.

Now is the time to live. In the prologue to his play, *The Time of Your Life*, William Saroyan said, "In the time of your life, live—" As he puts it, "In the time of your life, live—so that in that good time there shall be no ugliness or death for yourself or for any like you...In the time of your life, live—so that in that wondrous time you shall not add to the misery and sorrow of the world but shall smile to the infinite delight and mystery of it." For me, this statement captures the sense of awe and wonder for which we should strive. Recognizing you have a wondrous opportunity to partake of the joy and bounty and beauty of life, don't let it pass you by unsavored!

Questions to Put You on Track

Asking yourself some questions can help you put your life back in the living mode:

♦ If I knew what I know now about my present life situation, would I choose it over again if I had the chance?

♦ If ten years ago, when I began my career, I knew what I do now, would I choose the same career again?

♦ If I knew before I started with this relationship what I know now, would I choose to pursue it again?

These questions allow you to objectively reevaluate where you are now, to gauge whether your present course should continue or if changes are in order.

A second set of questions to ask is:

♦ I have these dreams and desires. If I keep doing what I'm doing now, can I expect to get where I want to be?

♦ Realistically, if I keep acting as I am now, will I enjoy a close marriage (or other goal) in the future?

♦ If I keep acting as I am now, can I expect to attain the career position (or other goal) I originally sought for myself?

These next two questions can illuminate any dull, boring or potentially harmful aspects of your life. They should stop you in your my tracks every time:

♦ Would I choose to do it over again?

♦ If I keep doing what I'm doing now, will I obtain the results I desire?

If the answer is "no" to either question, you have isolated an event or situation that needs to be changed. The beauty of these two questions is that you can be brutally honest with yourself. A "yes" or "no" is non-threatening. It only requires honesty with yourself. You are not making any promises or commitments to make any difficult changes; you're only asking yourself to evaluate a situation. The wonderful thing is that if you are willing to be honest with yourself, this two-question exercise will often give you the impetus to take the next little step, to ask the next little question, *"What can I do differently?"* This can lead to a whole new planning process and a whole new set of life adventures.

Remember, your existence now is not just a preparation for starting some future life. You are not *preparing* to live, you are living *now*! This is not a practice run. This is the real thing. Make the most of each moment. You can't go back and, at the snap of a finger, simply erase the effects of what you have done thus far.

"This is the time of my life. Am I having the time of my life?" This affirmation and question will provide the motivation to consider changing a part of your life that is obstructing the flow of happiness or give you the vitality to envision new dreams. Some of the predicaments in which you find yourself may not be readily solvable. Duty and loyalty, two qualities not very popular lately, may dictate that certain events cannot be eliminated. You may have children to support, which may preclude going off to live a life of carefree adventure or preclude abruptly quitting a less-than-satisfying position in your firm. However, other changes can be made. There are always some steps you can take now to allow for more far-reaching changes later that reaffirm, *now* is the time of your life!

> **TRANSFORMATION:**
>
> *Life is not preparation for some future event.*
>
> "I tell you, NOW is the time of God's favor, NOW is the day of salvation." (2 Corinthians 6:2)

Chance the Risk

Living is growing. You are living when you are growing or encouraging and allowing others to grow. What is growth but change, over time, in a positive direction? This is a trademark of life—change. With growth, we anticipate improvement, betterment. However, whenever we dare to change, one trade-off may be abandoning the security of current habits and circumstances in exchange for the expectation of improvement. Unfortunately, change does not guarantee improvement, but it is a requirement. So risk is involved, letting go of present, but perhaps limited, security but nonetheless security, with a hope for something better.

It's hope that inspires us to take a chance and risk being vulnerable and unprotected. Nature is filled with this recurring theme. We are all familiar with the metamorphosis of a caterpillar to a butterfly. To change—to grow—the caterpillar must become vulnerable in a stationary cocoon while the transformation process happens. This process of risk in exchange for growth is typical of many creatures in the physical world. Another good example is the lobster. In order for it to grow beyond its hard, secure shell it must risk shedding and leaving behind the limitations of its current shell while a new larger one grows. During the interim, the lobster is vulnerable without a protective covering. It may be at the mercy of other fish and ocean currents dashing it against the rocks and coral. However, it has no choice: If it is to go on growing, risk and vulnerability must be endured.

You, too, must risk your security and perhaps more. You may need to risk your present life order to really live. Are you willing to endure the vulnerability of a new environment, new experiences, to grow? The alternative is to endure the boredom and malaise of stagnation in order to clutch on to present perceived security. While the lobster has no choice, it's programmed to grow; you *can* choose. You're not forced to grow mentally, spiritually, or as an influence in the lives of those you touch. You have a choice. Really, though, there is not much of a choice when you think of it. You either clutch to a modicum of protection and slowly succumb to boredom and atrophy. Or you can risk present security and accept graciously the problems associated with change to experience new adventures.

Once you accept voluntary change, and the voluntary vulnerability that goes with it, you'll experience the joy and excitement of new adventure. Then you can beckon others onto the same

TRANSFORMATION:

Keep the mindset that risk is a requirement for growth.

When Jesus approached two men who would become his disciples, he said, "Come follow me and I will make you fishers of men...At once they left their nets and followed him."   (Matthew 4:19,20)

path. As you live a transforming, meaningful life, your example and encouragement can help others to accept risk. You are in actuality inviting others to live with you. Your own enthusiasm for life incites others to grow.

This is the progression: Willingness to risk, acceptance of change, then growth. And when you risk, you learn that problems are necessary prerequisites. But remember this: It's so much easier to endure pain or problems knowing there is a reason for them and that there is an end in sight. That end puts you on the next level of growth.

Really Knowing Yourself

Another major help to allay the fear that is connected with problems is to be clear about who you are, what you want, and where you are in your life quest. The more you know about yourself, the more you are aware of your assets and abilities that can be counted on when setbacks or major problems arise. I frequently find, though, that people, while knowing their physical and mental abilities, are not really aware of the *values* that motivate them. Recognizing these values and being able to specifically call on them when beset with difficulties is a major source of power. By values, I mean the concepts that are most important to you. These are the qualities and principles that you personally consider most dear. The concepts you stand for, believe in and seek.

Periodically, I assess my own needs and values, recognizing that they may change over time. Over the years, I have collected and revised a list of the beliefs that motivate me. I have used it as a reminder to stay in touch with those ideas that energize me and sustain me through difficulties. These are concepts that I believe, that I stand for, and that I'm willing to endure hardships for. For years I have carried with me a list of these values, a list that now amounts to twenty-two personal beliefs. This list includes such personal motivators as having a clear conscience before God, comprehending the wisdom of the ages and progressive enlightenment, experiencing a sense of self-respect and self-esteem, protecting my physical health, needing loving relationships, having the security of a close family, seeing evidence of personal growth in my life, and walking in the freedom of integrity. Further on I'll ask you to construct your own list of values.

Here's how I use my values. First, when a difficulty arises that could potentially be a long-term problem, I ask, "Is this problem something (based on my values) I choose to endure?" If it is, I am immediately bolstered and energized to endure. Since I have made the choice and I have decided it is worth my effort to stand firm, I am in control. I also assess whether a problem is germane to one of the priorities I have identified as a need or value. On the other hand, problems related to values not high on my list I relegate to second place and put on hold. Why waste time on something not essential and not having a high pay-back? For example, I have a friend who endured a job with high pressure only to later acknowledge the financial security it provided was not really a priority in his life. The problems he endured were needless. On the other hand, if you are a person with financial security high on your list of priorities just remind yourself, "This is important to me. I've chosen to accept these inconveniences because a priority need is involved." It's a lot easier to endure when you know you've made the choice. You're in control.

I know of someone who endured the abuse and ingratitude of an elderly parent. I asked Barb, "How do you put up with it?" She simply replied that this provided her with a sense that she was returning the care she was given when she was young, and this was important to her. The fact that her mother did not appreciate her efforts was immaterial. Barb wanted to do what was important to her. As a result, her endurance of ingratitude appeared effortless and had little affect on her vibrant enthusiasm. Having made a personal choice and acknowledging it made all the difference.

Scripture provides the encouragement, "As you know, we consider blessed those who have persevered. You have heard of Job's perseverance and have seen what the Lord finally brought about. The Lord is full of compassion and mercy." (James 5:11)

Remember though, that values and needs change over time. You will want to periodically reassess your personal values. You may be familiar with the works of Abraham Maslow and the "Hierarchy of Needs" he made famous. His research predicts that individuals committed to growth will follow an expected path motivated by progressive sets of needs. As one set of needs is fulfilled, another set arises to replace it as motivators. Realizing this, you'll not be surprised when the problems and pressures you had previously accepted as worth enduring are no longer of primary importance in your life. These old pressures can be eliminated in exchange for a new set of problems commensurate with your new priority needs. These five plateaus of need-motivation usually appear in this predictable order (though not necessarily):

(1) *Physiological needs*—self-preservation and the needs for food, shelter, sleep, and other physical requirements.

(2) *Safety needs*—security and a desire for a predictable, consistent environment that provides order and stability for our existence.

(3) *Belonging and loving needs*—affectionate relationships with people in general but specifically with significant others in one's life. These relationships include mutual trust and acceptance along with the giving and receiving of love.

(4) *Esteem needs*—self-respect, including confidence and competence based on achievement and independence, a feeling of deserved attention and respect from others.

(5) *Self-actualizing needs*—the desire for growth and development to become what we are capable of being, a feeling that we have fully utilized our talents and potentials.

Exchange Your Problems

When I was young, I started a janitorial business. Collecting money from customers with past-due accounts often proved to be a major problem, though the amounts were only $25 or $50. Years later when I managed a financial services business, my problem involved the collection of thousands of dollars in debts. Yet I had to admit, the earlier $25 and $50 problems, at the time, seemed much more imposing than the new set of problems were.

Remember, life never allows for elimination of problems if you are growing. You merely exchange one set of problems for a new set. As you grow, your problems become more complex, but through experience you gain the ability to meet these problems confidently. With wisdom, you are able to ignore needless problems or sidestep barriers not vital to your own need attainment, but problems will always loom.

Problems no longer will surprise or befuddle you. You will expect them and look on them as stepping stones to success. Problems form a pathway guiding you to success as you first encounter

> **TRANSFORMATION:**
>
> *A successful life does not mean elimination of problems but a selective acceptance of more complex problems that lead to more far-reaching goals.*
>
> "From everyone who has been given much, much will be demanded; and who has been entrusted with much, much more will be asked."
> (Luke 12:48)

them, creatively solve them, and then selectively move on to new ones. Merely ask, "Are these problems I'm beset by necessary to fulfill my needs? If so, I'm willing to meet them gladly for the rewards inherent in them."

Satisfaction Versus Dissatisfaction

Just as Maslow has helped us to see that the quest for continued growth is natural, we need to fight the other natural tendency to rest on our laurels and to seek security knowing that continued striving is required for continued fulfillment. If we are to grow, we must be dissatisfied with "good enough." You are required to choose between excellence and average, between "'good enough" and "the very best." Paradoxically, satisfaction with life comes only with selective dissatisfaction. The philosophy of just getting by will never serve you well. Learn to be dissatisfied with just any effort when you can attain a higher level.

It's easy to be content with being average. It's easy to think, "I'm doing as well as most." Have you ever thought, though, that average is just as close to the bottom as it is to the top?! In many ways we are programmed to be content with being average. We want to be like the majority. We are reluctant to stand out from the crowd in appearance or presence. However, there are some skills or abilities you possess that are crying to be used, pleading to have the chance to demonstrate that you are unique. Part of you is begging to experience the exhilaration of knowing that very few can do as well as you in your chosen endeavor. What a feeling of satisfaction to know you are contributing to society in your own special way, in a way unique to you!

Excellence, then, is the standard to be cultivated. You have an innate urge to seek and to grow toward excellence. Only by cultivating the desire for distinction will you be truly happy. On the one hand, society's standards are set rather low out of necessity to encourage conformity and unity. It's up to you to see how you can go beyond that standard to set a personal standard for yourself. Another word for "average" is "mediocre." Many people are satisfied with a mediocre life, satisfied with just getting by. Why be content with being average, a place where you are precariously perched between "second rate" and excellent, when just a little bit of extra effort will produce the extraordinary? In every field, such a small distance separates the winners from the losers, the champions from the "also-rans." In most foot races (for example, the 100-meter dash), the difference in time between first and eighth place is usually a mere one-tenth of a second. In so much of life, this is true. Just that little bit of extra effort that comes from striving for excellence will set you apart from the pack, for your satisfaction and for the benefit of society.

Cultivate the standard of excellence by:

- ♦ Being dissatisfied with the mediocre or average
- ♦ Being willing to act, willing to do more than what is just acceptable
- ♦ Cultivating confidence in your abilities and uniqueness
- ♦ Being willing to take risks

Problems

Whenever I am beset with problems, I go through a mental checklist, reminding myself of the basics in which I believe. When mentally low, I remind myself of some of the basic tenets I would readily accept were it not for my temporary low mental state. I have written basic principles I accept without question. I've analyzed these and meditated on them in an environment free of problems. Then, when problems do occur, and I understandably don't have the propensity toward optimism, I can remind or refresh myself with these ideas. I can say, "Though I know it's hard for me to accept this now, I do believe, have proved to myself, and have faith that if only I adhere to these principles, all will work out."

When you are overcome with problems, hold onto this: problems are temporary, not permanent. Problems are short-term *en route* to long-term success. What is more, problems are actually stepping stones leading to long-term victory. These unexpected impediments to success are, in fact, necessary to future fulfillment.

A friend told me the most valuable lesson she learned from her divorce was that she will never allow her happiness to be dependent on the whim of someone else. Only after the divorce did she realize that her day-to-day contentment had depended on her husband's mood and his ever-changing opinion of her. When things weren't going well at the office, he'd take it out on her. When she didn't fulfill a task exactly as he wanted, she allowed herself to suffer from his animosity for days. After the divorce, Joan promised herself she'd never again allow her disposition to be dependent on someone else's mood or opinion. She, of course, wished she hadn't had to go through the pain of a divorce, but she admitted she learned a valuable lesson from the ordeal that would serve her the rest of her life.

I have carried away something positive from every difficulty I have encountered. At a time when you're in a positive mood, review past problems—jobs from which you have been laid off, health maladies you've had, or friends you've lost. Haven't you at least learned something from each such encounter? Can't you say the experience has been valuable? Aren't you a more experienced and stronger person because of the difficulty? The answer is inevitably, "Yes!"

TRANSFORMATION:

We learn something of value from every problem in life we're forced to encounter.

"We were under great pressure, far beyond our ability to endure...But this happened that we might not rely on ourselves, but on God." (2 Corinthians 1:8,9)

At the moment you may not have the time to step back and see the positive aspect. Once I went camping in the mountains. When I arrived it was cloudy, rainy, cold, and disappointing. I was depressed and ready to turn back. However, the next morning the weather changed, and then I saw I was in the midst of unsurpassed beauty with snow-capped mountain peaks around me. I had been fooled by the temporary clouds and rain. The same is true with most difficulties. At the time, the positive element may not be apparent—but it becomes clear later. When life's fog and rain stops, you then realize what you've gone through. The positive factor always materializes. When I have problems, I just remind myself, "This will end. I'll be able to discern the beauty tomorrow."

Activity

List several mistakes and several set-backs
you have endured in the past.

Now, for each of these, what have you learned
and what have you gained from the experience?

List also the good that came from the problem.

Can you admit to yourself that something worthwhile
has always come from the problems, even if only that
you have learned a valuable lesson that
could help you in the future?

Crisis Coping

In times of crisis, remind yourself first that any problem will be short-term in the sense that there is always a way to cope. You need only look for the solution. Each failure is an investment in the future. Life is a learning process, so look for constructive feedback from the challenge rather than let your imagination run away with a list of all the possible negative results. A greater number of positive outcomes is also possible.

My wife, Marlene, had such a crisis not long ago. In a short time she lost both her father, through illness, and her brother, by suicide. There are few experiences more devastating. Sorrow, regret, anger, powerlessness, and the emotions of past childhood crises all hit her at once. I felt powerless to help. All I could do was be there. I knew she had to work things through on her own. All I could say, and I repeated it often, was, "This will end, but you've got to follow it through." She had a dream that her original family might one day be the family she so much longed for while growing up. Now it would never be.

Patiently working it through, coping as best she could, keeping busy so she wasn't enveloped terminally with the sorrow, she emerged a stronger and wiser person. She learned to cope with the finality of death, she learned to trust her faith, she learned to treasure her present life possibilities. These valuable lessons may not have been understood any other way. Now she's the first to testify that the rewards were worth the travail.

When confronted with a crisis, I suggest coping this way:

(1) Remind yourself each challenge is actually an opportunity for personal growth. You will feel stronger as a result of the experience. Look for the good. *Optimism pays.*

(2) Take one step at a time. Do what you can at the moment. Don't feel you must resolve the whole problem or have all the answers at once. Do what is necessary to cope with the immediate crisis. Answers will always follow with the details.

(3) Take action. Do something. Keep busy. Don't allow yourself idle time to allow your imagination to wallow in negative imaginings.

(4) Recognize your resources. You don't have to face the difficulty totally on your own. You have relatives, friends, work mates, neighbors, and club or church associates that you can ask for help. An emergency always brings out the best in people. There will always be someone who can help.

(5) Remember, it's not the exact strategy that is important. There are many ways to resolve a difficulty. What is important is the commitment to persevere.

(6) Finally, remember *you're not alone.* You have the solemn promise of the most powerful force in the universe. "See, the Sovereign Lord comes with power, and his arm rules for him. See, his reward is with him." (Isaiah 40:10)

Napoleon Hill used to say, "Each adversity carries with it the seed of a greater good."

Two Parting Thoughts

Time is never wasted; it's never too late. If you come to a realization even on your proverbial deathbed, that is a new beginning. Start where you are. Don't worry about past opportunities that have been squandered. Now is what counts. This moment, do what you can now. I have had friends berate themselves lamenting, "If only I knew then what I know now." I tell them that's the wonderful thing—you *do* know *now*, even if it took a wretched experience to teach you. Some people go through life never knowing what you do *now*. Be thankful and use what you've learned now! I firmly believe it's never too late. Even if you wait till your final few breaths to make peace with yourself and with others, even just to say, "I'm sorry," or "I couldn't do it all," or "I'm sorry I didn't get it right the first time." That's a victory and a solution of sorts. "I'm sorry I didn't get it right. Can I have another chance?" Who knows? Perhaps you can!

Surveying the history of the Roman Empire from the vantage point of time, philosopher and historian Will Durant concluded, "Rome remained great as long as she had enemies who forced her to unity, vision, and heroism. When she had overcome all her enemies, she flourished for a moment and then began to die."

Need I say more? Be thankful for your problems, your enemies, and your dilemmas. They provide the inspiration for all that is noble in humanity!

"Art is unthinkable without risk and spiritual self-sacrifice."
(Boris Pasternak)

"I consider that our present sufferings are not worth comparing with the glory that will be revealed in us." (Romans 8:18)

CHAPTER 3

Goal-Growing

Few things in life are as powerful as a burning desire. Let me tell you about one of my ambitious goals. One day I decided I was going to earn a Ph.D. in social psychology. That may not necessarily sound ambitious, but when you consider I invented this goal when I was in my thirties, I had a full-time job with a family, including three children to support, and had earned no college degree or credentials up to that point, it was ambitious.

This goal was a burning desire, and even though I didn't know at the time how much effort would be required, I consciously continued to keep this goal alive. I took one step at a time, assessing first which subjects I could get college credits for based on my work experience and which subjects I knew sufficiently well to take final exams with a minimum of home study. When difficulties arose like finding time for class, study and family after a full day at work, I created inventive solutions. I learned to carry my textbooks with me whenever I thought I might have to wait at an appointment or while my wife was shopping. I always carried some school project in my car, so when I'd have free time for lunch, I'd spend uninterrupted time away from the office at a restaurant studying.

At times I was discouraged. One time I thought I had only a final dissertation left to meet my goal, only to be informed I was still required to prepare for and pass two two-day comprehensive exams before going further. A research project took two years longer than I had expected, but I kept going, and I did attain my goal. With goal-setting as you will learn it here, it's nearly impossible to fail!

Sometimes Christians seem hesitant to dare to believe that they can accomplish meaningful things in their lives. Somehow they feel it presumptuous to think they can do something great, as if such an act would be denying their subservient position before God. That's not what God wishes. He wants you to succeed.

He wants you to do meaningful things, great things. He only asks that "whatever you do, do it all for the glory of God." (1 Corinthians 10:31) What great things could you accomplish if you really believe you have the greatest power in the universe working to assure your success?

Goal-setting needs to become second nature to you. It's not difficult, but life success is inextricably linked to goal success. Also for you to feel in control, there must be a sense of mastery, a feeling that you are not at the mercy of outside forces. Goal-setting and goal attainment allow you to feel in control, one of the basic tenets of mental health in a fully functioning person. Goal-setting that will make fulfillment of your dreams much easier than you thought possible.

There are few areas of practical living on which the Bible is more explicit than the insistence on setting and attaining goals. In fact, one of the major reasons Christian countries throughout history have raised their standards of living far above others is their setting and attaining goals. "Keep your eyes on the prize" is a frequent refrain among Christians. We have ultimate spiritual goals, but the Bible stresses living by a set of goals in everyday life. "A man reaps what he sows." (Galatians 6:7)

Learning to set goals, learning to work incrementally toward the attainment of goals, and acquiring a general goal orientation about life are absolutely essential to a more fulfilling life. The process is simple. Once you decide specifically what you want and acknowledge that the desire is very important to you, you have set a goal. Then you agree on the steps necessary for attainment and agree to follow those steps, to see the goal come to fruition.

A number of different techniques have worked for me over the years. You are certain to discover one or two ideas that will improve your goal setting ability and provide the extra stimulus needed to follow through on these goals. If you are a veteran goal setter, great! You'll find some helpful suggestions here. But I'm going to cover basics in case you aren't accustomed to goal-setting.

By all means, dare to believe. President Jimmy Carter was asked why he had run for the presidency, why he felt he was qualified. He said, "I really didn't think I was qualified until I met the other candidates, and then I knew I was as qualified as anyone else." He dared to believe it was possible, and he worked methodically to reach that goal.

The First Big Step

You can have anything you want in life if you will just write it down! This is not an exaggeration. In almost all cases it's an absolute fact. Life is a wonderful smorgasbord of opportunities. So many possibilities are there for the choosing. The initial step is to simply settle on what it is you really want. Everyone daydreams about possibilities. Our minds are fertile with ideas, but I'm talking about something very different from daydreaming. The initial difference between a daydreamer and a goal setter is the act of making a decision. A decision—"This is what I want"—is articulated. The decision becomes a concrete resolution once it is *written down*!

With any goal, the steps are as simple—or as complicated—as:

(1) Daydreaming of the possibilities

(2) Deciding which of the possibilities you will seek to attain

(3) Fixing that decision in your being by writing it down

Writing is so critical because it takes effort. That first effort demonstrates a certain amount of commitment by the seeker. The daydreamer enjoys his romp through the fertile pastures of the mind but never gets around to the business at hand. A written statement is that initial gesture that you will make a commitment to do the work necessary for goal realization. A written statement is tantamount to planting a seed. For a seed to germinate, it first must be planted. Writing down your goal plants that thought in your mind and being. Then you nurture the seed, and it takes root and grows.

Probably the most inspiring and graphic example of the power of goal-setting is John Goddard's story. At the age of fifteen, John made a dream list of what he wished to accomplish in his life.

Included were adventures, such as climbing mountains—Kilimanjaro, and the Matterhorn—and actually following the original exploration paths of Marco Polo and Alexander the Great. Other more conventional goals included reading various great works of literature, marrying and having children, and visiting every country of the world. All totaled, John had 127 diverse dreams. However, they were more than just wishes; he wrote them down and really believed he could accomplish them. They were clear, sharp dreams. As a result, John Goddard, by his sixties, had been able to fulfill well over 100 of these, including kayaking the 4,000 miles of the Nile River from its source. He is a veteran of numerous expeditions, safaris, and adventures and continues to work toward the fulfillment of the rest of these goals. He extols the power of goal-setting and has proven with his own life that you can do virtually anything you dream. He says, "I set up a blueprint of goals so that I would always have something to work for. I was also aware of people around me who had gotten into ruts, had never taken risks, never challenged themselves in any way. I was determined not to go that route."

I can't stress this point enough. As simple as writing something down sounds, it's absolutely essential if you want to realize your goals. As you go through this book and recognize an idea you want to incorporate in your life, *write it down*! Once you realize an

> **TRANSFORMATION:**
>
> *Solidify a daydream into a real-world reality by writing it down.*

action is necessary for your growth, *write it down*! If you discover a way of life you wish to master, *write it down*! The act of writing fixes the idea in your mind. A nebulous impulse or an initial thought takes a material form when it is written. An idea is just a ghost of a thought. But that ghost can be solidified and literally seen with just the stroke of a pen.

To write something, you must first put it into words. Putting it into words requires the mental process of thinking and choosing the specific words you need to "flesh out" your idea. That additional mental process generates the energy inherent in goal statements. Believe it. You can have whatever you want if you first take the initiative to *write it down.*

Some of the most startling and satisfying experiences in my life have occurred when I've come across long-lost notes I'd written years before, containing lists of goals and resolves I'd made to myself. As I scanned the lists, I realized that without exception every goal I had set had come to fruition without seemingly any further effort on my part. It thrilled me to realize that ideas I had once upon a time and thought important enough to write down had come true! One list I found had included the goals of buying a house in the country, publishing a specific research paper in an academic journal, and finding a new teaching position. One by one I was able to check them off. It surprised me to discover many goals on my lists to which I had never consciously given another thought, and yet I had attained them. The act of writing down those goals fixed them in my subconscious, and my subconscious mind guided me to the reality. Write down your goals in detail. You, too, may have the unexpected pleasure of one day finding buried notes of goal lists and be exhilarated to exclaim, "This, that I wrote down long ago, has been fulfilled and I have, in fact, gone far beyond that seed of an idea!"

Planting the Seed

Another important facet in goal-setting is in the "soil" where you plant your goal seeds. When you understand you're already a success once you write your goal down, you're planting in fertile soil. That's right, success is a process, not an end result. Success is experienced as you act, not just when you have completed the action. I am successful because I make the effort to conceive and then act. So deciding on a dream and "just knowing" it's going to come true is the fertile soil in which you always want to plant your goal seeds. Most people will dream but will not take the steps to make those dreams come true. You distinguish yourself from the majority by taking this initial step, not just daydreaming, but putting your dreams into material form, then exclaiming, "I am a success because I am taking, without doubting, the steps necessary for fulfillment of my life goals." You have confidence that the goal seed will germinate. As the Bible says, "A man reaps what he sows." (Galatians 6:7)

Goal Philosophy

All life is goal-oriented. Even the lowest forms of life have goals—survival and proliferation. It's only in higher life forms that goals are not fully programmed in the organism. We have choices. Having choices is a blessing which can feel like a curse if we have never been taught to seize the opportunity.

So, dream dreams. Let your mind soar with visions. You can never have too many goals! Just remember one very important thing when setting your goals: Be specific. A desire to have more money is an admirable goal, but it's vague. Writing it down will almost certainly assure its success, but how much money is "more?" A windfall of a hundred dollars fulfills that goal of more money, but that's probably not what the dreamer had in mind. Be clear. "I see myself attaining a savings of $100,000 three years from now," is a more well-defined goal. Having a better family life is also a worthy goal, but exactly what does that mean? Be clear and concise. Does this mean having a harmonious relationship with all family members and living in an environment where all can express themselves without continual bickering? Does it mean being able to provide a stable environment for your children's growth? Does it mean being able to provide all the material necessities that will assure family members a sense of security? Again, be specific!

Not long ago when I discovered I have a minor heart problem, I set as a goal to switch to a vegetarian diet. I realized if I were going to live consistently by it, I had to be very clear why I was adopting this drastic lifestyle and what it would mean. After researching the possible approaches to healthy eating, I specifically established what "vegetarian" would mean to me. I would eat only grains, fruits, and vegetables with no meat, fish, or poultry. I would also eat no-fat cheese and skim milk products. I resolved to eliminate fast food and restaurant fare. I specifically wrote down changes I'd have to make and why they were important to me. I decided how I'd handle lunches with clients and academic banquets. I even carried a picture of a trim, healthy runner to remind me what I wished to accomplish. One year later I was still living my new lifestyle.

Specificity imprints an indelible goal impression on the subconscious mind. As you meditate on the specifics of your goals, you see a clear picture of what you desire. That "snapshot" serves as a picture for your subconscious mind to work toward. When setting the goal, a detailed plan of how the goal will be fulfilled is not necessary. That will come in time. Your subconscious mind will see to the details. What is important at this time is that you form the picture as clearly and concisely and with as much detail as possible. A new silver BMW sedan with black leather interior is much more effective than just a new BMW as a motivational picture. Etching that goal in your conscious mind brands the picture in your subconscious mind. All texts on goal-setting will tell you this. What is not often mentioned, however, is the order and probability of when these goals will materialize.

We can have hundreds of goals simultaneously, I know people with five to six hundred goals. Having so many may not allow for resolution time for their fulfillment since we have a finite lifetime. However, your goals will be fulfilled in direct proportion to their meaning to you. To the extent that you are motivated and excited about a goal, its fulfillment is assured. This is not stressed enough in goal-planning and accounts for why many people have never found goal-setting effective. People frequently say, "It just doesn't work for me." I ask them several questions: Did you write it down? Were you specific? Was it something you were excited about? Did you feel enthusiasm flowing through your veins every time you thought of the idea? If you wrote it down, it will probably happen, but if you're excited about it and sustain that enthusiasm, it will most assuredly happen—and much sooner.

The secret, then, is to formulate the goal in such a way that it elicits excitement when you think of it. If thoughts of this goal do *not* make you excited, you can be sure this is not really a high priority goal and will not enjoy high priority attainment. In general, the more specific the goal, the more powerful the surge of excitement it produces. So when you write a goal, ask yourself, "Does it really excite me?" If not, rephrase the goal statement until it produces a surge of electricity within you. Losing ten pounds is a great goal, but you may not be excited when you contemplate the pain of denial. Such a goal is doomed to be sabotaged by your subconscious mind. Recognizing this, you, as a veteran goal setter, will meditate further till the goal is reworded in such a way as to generate a spark of enthusiasm. "I see myself with the self-confidence that comes from being proud of my appearance which losing ten pounds will insure." Now that may provide the spark of motivation that excites you! If not, reword and rework it further, till you feel the spark.

Forming goals and writing them down are like collecting the wood and material to start a fire. This preparation is the critical first step. However, nothing will happen until the materials are set afire. Enthusiasm is that spark that ignites the fire. At times, just a small spark of enthusiasm is adequate, but a flaming match will assuredly kindle a roaring fire.

If it still doesn't have the spark of enthusiasm you need, set it aside for awhile, and let the idea incubate. Come back to it later. Remember that this goal may be important to you, but if it is not exciting to you, you may as well move on to something else since it just won't happen anytime soon.

> **TRANSFORMATION:**
>
> *Reword your goal statements till they produce excitement within you.*
>
> "...eager (zealous) to do what is good." (Titus 2:14)

This is true especially if it's a complicated plan that will take great effort. The goals that cause enthusiasm to well up in you are the ones that will come to pass soon. I've often found that if an idea is important but not very exciting to me, I still won't give up on it. I simply realize that this goal may be longer in coming than others. However, if I mull it over and let the idea grow, I'm usually able to restate it later in terms that excite. The idea is suddenly transformed. It's no longer just a possibility. It's a probability, because I waited until I could couch the idea in terms that generated strong positive emotions in me. This suggestion in goal-setting is often overlooked. It's much better to have a few personally exciting goals than to have hundreds of half-hearted daydreams. We've all known people who say, "It would be nice to have this or that." But we can almost be sure they'll never attain those things because of the lukewarm manner in which they speak about their desires. Without strong motivation, the goal is impotent.

Activity

Knowing that it's important to differentiate deep-seated goals from wishful dreams, take time to ask yourself several "what if" questions.

What if you were told you had one year to live?
What would you want to do during that last year?
List at least five or six desires.

Next, imagine that eleven of those twelve months had elapsed and you had but one month to live.
What would you do now?
Again, list five or six things.

Finally, what if providence granted you only several days more to live?
How would your list change?

Now go back and scrutinize your list. Can you see the activities listed are evidently your deep-seated basic desires?

This list helps you discover what is *really* important to you. These goals already have an emotional impetus associated with them. Take advantage of the discovery. If you question which goals you should start with, these three lists will direct you. You may wish to include some of these items in your initial goal list. As long as those items are clearly stated and written down, they most certainly will be among the very first goals the built-in, goal-seeking mechanism in your mind will process. Your very being yearns for these.

The Goal Stepladder

You've set a major goal, but it seems too monumental ever to accomplish. Don't be discouraged. The next step is dividing the goal into smaller subgoals. Now the task is less formidable. The goal no longer appears to be beyond our abilities to accomplish.

Next, these subgoals can be divided into "bite-sized" pieces that can be readily achieved. As each of these incremental steps is accomplished, you (the goal setter) will feel a sense of power and fulfillment that energizes you to tackle the next step toward realization.

I've had people tell me years later, "This is one thing you taught me that helped so much." A lot of people get so disheartened by a huge task that they're discouraged before they even start and keep putting off doing it. If they can plan one tiny step, one they know they can easily finish, they'll get it done. For example, if you are determined to write a new resume to pursue a career change, the first step may be to find your old resume today. The next step may be to make notes on what changes you feel need be made. Next, decide who will type this for you. Each stage is non-threatening and simple.

> **TRANSFORMATION:**
>
> *A formidable goal is conquered by dividing it into progressive, simple steps — divide and conquer.*

Whenever a goal appears too formidable, begin to divide it. Then subdivide further until you arrive at a starting point you can easily attain today. Writing a novel may at first seem to be an impossible task, but when it's incrementally divided, the discouragement evaporates. A novel can be divided into chapters. Each chapter is merely a short story. Each short story consists of an introduction, a body, and a conclusion. Perhaps before the chapters can be written, background research needs to be done. Even before that, some basic ideas for the novel need to be decided on. That's something that can be started today. Now you have broken down the complex goal of writing a novel to a starting point you can begin and complete in one sitting. Then if research needs to be done, start with a list of sources necessary to consult. Consult them one at a time. These are all small subgoals, each easily accomplished. As each one is completed and checked off, you are energized to tackle the next step. Personal energy thrives on the achievement of even a minor task. The exhilaration that comes from successfully completing one task empowers you to take the next step.

Incremental goal-setting is a necessity for any long-range project. Business planners have long known the usefulness of distinguishing between long-range and short-range projects. Both are important. A long-term view for your future consists of related short-term projects.

You can easily work on several goals at once. In fact, to be successful in all eight aspects of life, you need goals in each. Have both long-range and short-term goals in each area of your life. Goals in the areas of physical health, family orientation, and career accomplishment can be dealt with simultaneously. As long as each picture you hold has incremental goals, they can all be attained in unison. Frequently, you'll find many of these areas of life are related in the sense that progress in one area leads to progress in another. A goal achieved in the physical fitness area can simultaneously lead to fulfillment of a career goal, for example. As your health improves, the more energy you have to devote to your career. With improved health, you experience less fatigue in late morning and late afternoon. Hence these hours are recaptured for career advancement.

While having a number of goals is essential for growth, many successful people find that having one central goal highlighted at a time is most beneficial. This provides an overall orientation for your personal life. When I was introduced to goal-setting in my early twenties, I recognized that my central goal was to become a fully-functioning adult—a good husband and a good father. In my late twenties, that central orientation became the building of a business, subjugating my other desires till this one major goal was fulfilled. Later I made my education my consuming passion. Next I longed to establish myself academically, teaching at a college level and publishing my research work. Now my desire to share what I've learned has become my major focus. Each central goal has, in turn, given me a reference by which to arrange other goals and activities to complement my current major goal project.

Habit Goals

Frequently one finds that a particular goal requires forming new habits. When this is true, take heart in the research findings of behavioral psychologists. Studies have found it takes approximately twenty-one days to replace one habit with a new one. It really works! It has always given me extra confidence when I embark on the formation of a new habit to know I need only put up with the inconvenience or irritation that may be associated with a major change if it's only for a limited time. I remind myself that I can put up with just about anything for three weeks if I know there is an end in sight.

Let's say you set a goal to read for thirty minutes every day in your career field. Assure yourself that the extra effort and inconvenience of forcing yourself to comply will last, at most, three weeks. At the end of that period the new habit becomes ingrained, and you will adhere to it with little conscious effort. The first few days may be difficult, but it becomes easier. By writing down the new habit you want to acquire on your daily "to-do" list, after about three weeks you'll no longer need to make a special effort to remember the new goal. It will have become a regular habit. This technique can be used for every area of your life, from establishing a congenial personality to eating in a more healthful manner; from developing more productive work habits to allocating more time for a vocational interest.

I recently formed the habit of not eating after supper, for example. The first few days were difficult I'll admit. I had gotten into the bad habit of snacking at night on popcorn or a small dessert. Even though it was nothing heavy, my weight was beginning to creep up. I was specific in forming my new habit. I wrote, "I will take only liquids after dinner or after 7 p.m." When writing goals, state them as a positive statement, not a negative one. For example, if I write, "I will not eat after 7 p.m.," this is difficult to accomplish since it's a confusing goal. I would not be directing my subconscious mind to do something but to not do something. That's ambivalent. The positive statement, "I will always eat my final meal each day before 7 p.m. and will take only liquids after dinner," is easier to visualize. That's what I did. I told myself, "I'm prepared for the first few days of difficulty and the next week or two of inconvenience to form a good habit." Every time I found myself rebelling I'd just say, "I can put up with anything for three weeks!" Sure enough, after three weeks the habit was formed. It no longer took any effort.

Goal Ladder Reclimbed

Here are the steps for successful goal achievement that I have found to work:

(1) Write out a simple statement of your goal or mission.

(2) Realistically assess the level of emotional involvement you have with this goal. Ask, "What is my level of commitment?" If it is not all-important, carrying a high level of emotional appeal, be honest with yourself. It's not really a goal; it's a wish.

(3) Write down the steps necessary to make this goal come true. List what must be done in order of accomplishment,

simply and without complication. This is your plan of action and will include the information you need to gather, the people you need to consult, and possible contingency plans if you become stuck at any level along the way.

(4) Set a realistic timetable for accomplishment; for example, having $10,000 in your bank account by a certain specific date.

(5) Begin with item one on your step list with what can be done today (or tomorrow at the latest). The first step must be very tiny so you have no trouble fulfilling it and can thereby start the momentum building for accomplishment.

(6) Assess regularly your progress and check off each step as it is fulfilled. Assessment also means flexibility. Don't be afraid to revise your goal or the steps to attain it if necessary.

(7) Once one goal is achieved, pause to bask in the joy of attainment and either have a new goal in mind or immediately begin the process of setting a new goal series.

This process should be a continual, revolving practice in all life areas and throughout life.

Your Control

I can't emphasize enough the fact that you have control over the most important elements in your goal success. You may not have control over the people around you or the environment in which you find yourself. You may not be able to control others' reception of your requests for help. However, the three most important ingredients are completely in your control. That's why it's nearly impossible to fail. These three important ingredients are:

♦ Carrying a vivid goal picture (visualization)

♦ The passion you feel about your goal

♦ The time you spend working toward your goal

You control these three major variables in goal-setting. To the extent you use these three factors and work with them, success is inevitable. So paint a crystal-clear picture of what you want in all details. First, though, choose a goal you can be excited about. Then frequently spend time either thinking about or actually working toward your goal. These are the important predictors of your success, and they're all in your control!

> **TRANSFORMATION:**
>
> *We have complete control over the most important variables that determine whether a goal comes true. That's why it's impossible to fail.*
>
> "Remember this: Whoever sows sparingly, reaps sparingly, and whoever sows generously, reaps generously." (2 Corinthians 9:6))

Don't waste your time on goals you cannot state specifically, including what you stand to gain and what you may need to sacrifice. A nebulous picture without details will never galvanize you to action. It's far better to save your energy for a project that is clearly seen and generates strong emotions.

Power Over Fear

Frequently, inspiring goals are left by the wayside due to fear of failure. This negative emotion, the opposite of the positive emotion needed to sustain goal attainment, is the force that prevents success. The best definition for fear I have found is, "Fear is the emotional response to a perceived threat."

Much of the debilitating power of fear is eliminated once we realize what fear is. Fear is a warning system. Once fear is detected, first ask, "Is the perceived threat real or imaginary?" Fear can be a great thing if it warns us of impending danger, but it can cripple us if our perception is of danger when in actuality the danger is illusory. So when fear hits, first sort out your feelings. Ask, "Is the emotion of fear present because I am encountering a new experience or stepping beyond my comfort zone?" That's not a valid reason to remain fearful. Is fear present because there is the possibility you might fail and be ridiculed? That, too, is not a valid reason for fear. Venturing into the unknown is not valid reason to allow fear to grow. So test the fears. Defining the fear and the basis of your specific emotional response to a given situation will strip fear of much of its power. When you understand why you feel threatened, you are able to deal with the issue. Often just by putting a fear into words can cause much of its negative power to dissipate. It no longer is all-encompassing. You have made it specific, and you can begin to see how to eliminate it.

You may have the fear of speaking to an audience. Rather than say, "I have always had this problem," ask yourself, "Why do I have this extreme fear while others don't? Is it because I fear making a fool of myself? Is it because I feel I don't know the topic well enough? Is it the fear of doing something different?" Once you come to a plausible explanation, it's much easier to handle. Now formulate a plan to confront the fear. Perhaps you can start by speaking to two or three people you know reasonably well, maybe first speaking while sitting down in front of a small group. Then look for an opportunity to speak before several other people you don't know. In time the fear becomes easier to handle since you've broken it into increments that are less threatening.

The first time I was going to teach a college level course, I analyzed my fear. For me it was just the fear of doing something strange. "How could I let the fear of the unknown hamper me from attempting what could be a major directional change in my life?" I asked. Putting the fear into words made it easier to confront. I decided to teach, but resolved to teach a subject in which I was very well-versed for my first course. Then I wrote down why the goal was important to me—what I hoped to accomplish by teaching a college course. I then asked other professors for suggestions on how they taught the class in the past. With these step-by-step preparations, the fear was overwhelmed by activity. As it turned out, I loved teaching, and it has been a constant delight to share my experiences with students eager to learn.

Probably the best antidote to fear of a new project is to insist on taking at least one small step forward in spite of trepidation. Divide the major goal into as many minor goals as possible. The smaller the steps, the less threatening they become. So much of fear is due to the apprehension of going beyond our comfort zone, going beyond what is familiar and habitual to us. By taking a tiny step at a time, the fear evaporates or at least becomes manageable. Fortunately, the more immense the project, the more small steps into which it can be divided, each undertaken with minimal apprehension.

Earlier, we discussed dividing goals into small increments. You now see this is beneficial for two reasons. Small steps are more manageable and more easily negotiated. But perhaps even more important, small steps help to dissipate the fear of the unknown and the fear of failure.

So what goals will you dare to accomplish? I have a friend who dared to believe he could be financially independent in five years even after he had sunk into the mire of poverty and had only a high school education. He borrowed a suit and went for an interview seeking a position as a manufacturer's representative for machine products. He knew nothing of machine products, but he was convinced he could learn. His sheer enthusiasm was enough to convince the personnel manager to give him a chance. He then spent long hours first studying the products thoroughly and then planning intensively. Daily he'd work well into the night writing up orders after a full day of canvassing. It wasn't easy, but he knew exactly what he wanted and reminded himself daily of his promise to himself. Though small, his first commission checks gave him proof his dream could materialize.

TRANSFORMATION:

Fear is a useful warning system, but first ask, "Is this fear real or imaginary?"

"For you did not receive a spirit that makes you a slave again to fear." (Romans 8:15)

Even after the first year when he was making a comfortable income, his goal sight was not lost. Later he met with a financial planner to prepare a savings program that would lead to financial independence. This, too, he followed diligently. The last time I met him he confided that his seemingly impossible dream was a reality.

Unexpected Help

The greater the project, the greater the sense of mission you experience and the greater the attraction of possible supporters to your cause. A project that has others helping you is more apt to come to completion. Remember a monumental goal that will have a beneficial effect for you may provide a considerable benefit to others, too. These others can be persuaded to participate. Simply formulate your goal in such a way that it will affect others positively, allow them to feel a sense of mission toward the project, and others will inevitably be attracted.

Enthusiasm is contagious. For example, as a manager, you can easily state your business growth or efficiency goal in such a way that the whole department will benefit. That way you pick up their support. Monumental charity goals have been reached by an organizer simply stating a goal in such a way that many others identify with and desire to become part. Don't be afraid to dream great dreams. If those monumental dreams are formulated to include others and they are welcomed, they'll share some of the responsibility to lighten your load. Never underestimate the power inherent in a great dream!

Review

We've covered a lot of ground, let's crystallize the major points so we don't lose them. These can be used as a checklist whenever a new goal is anticipated. Ask yourself the following:
Have I...

♦ written the goal down?

♦ worded the goal very specifically?

♦ set a time limit for accomplishment?

♦ tested the goal to be sure it's emotionally stimulating?

♦ divided the goal into small increments?

♦ promised to stick with it for at least three weeks (especially if it's a goal habit)?

♦ confronted my fear by analyzing why it's felt?

♦ regularly measured or tracked my progress?

Inspirational Thoughts

"Whatever the mind of man can conceive and believe it can achieve." (Napoleon Hill)

"Ask and it will be given to you; seek and you will find; knock and the door will be opened to you." (Matthew 7:7)

CHAPTER 4

Body Basics (Fitness)

One morning I sat down for breakfast. The next thing I knew, my wife was shaking me. I had blacked out without warning. Marlene was terrified, and I was more than a little concerned. I was only in my mid-twenties, much too young for a heart attack, I thought. That day I went to the doctor and anxiously awaited the results of various tests. In a few days I got the results, which indicated I had hypoglycemia, or low blood sugar. At times, the sugar in my blood was so low that not enough vital energy (sugar-fuel) was getting to my brain. Fortunately for me, this episode taught me a great deal about my body and taught me never to take for granted the seemingly effortless job it does to insure uninterrupted health. I had to restructure my eating habits to limit sugar and plan my meals and snack times. I couldn't go long between meals to take in the fuel that would be converted to blood sugar.

Through this experience, I learned not to take physical health for granted. I began to appreciate how my body provided me with warning signs, coaxing me to give it better care. This internal alarm system had alerted me with headaches and periods of lethargy. If I had responded to my body's request for regular quality fuel, I would have avoided a medical emergency. Since then I have realized optimum health is a privilege. I've continued to learn more about my particular idiosyncrasies and how to nurture the body that carries me through life.

It's so easy to focus on success and our spiritual goals that we ignore our physical health, as I did. Scripture gives the proper perspective to physical health. The Word says, "The body is the Temple of the Holy Spirit." (1 Corinthians 6:19) Your body is the instrument that allows you to sense and interact with the world. If you are to succeed in your endeavors, you need to give attention to your physical health. The absence of health can severely hamper your success.

Your physical well-being also affects every other aspect of life. Invariably when you take control of your health, you will feel much better and have much more quality time for activities. You'll also be more efficient in your career. You'll find yourself saying, "I didn't realize how tired I used to be and how much less energy I had before I made changes in my life."

I recall how I used to be enervated by late in the afternoon. I felt like sleeping and lacked the motivation to continue with a task, even when I was in my teens and twenties. Years later, I can look back with a sense of satisfaction that my energy level has improved.

These are exciting times. Daily, new discoveries are being made that help us achieve and maintain total fitness. Understanding the intricacies of the human body has advanced immeasurably in the last thirty years. Especially in the last five years we have witnessed milestones in the health-care profession. One can take control of his or her health. Understanding a few basic health attitudes will make a great difference in your physical well-being. Become familiar with these principles and practice them; you will notice an immediate improvement in your health. These are major attitude shifts about health that have gained acceptance in the last few years. They will help you reach your goal of self-improvement since they emphasize the things you can do for yourself to insure optimum health.

Physical health affects every other aspect of life. Vibrant health is an asset for career advancement and enables one to feel fully alive hours longer each day. Optimum health retrieves that extra hour or two of time for study and meditation or provides an extra hour or two of fully awake time to dedicate to enjoyable activities. Indeed, emotional and mental well-being are tied directly to physical health. With such far-reaching benefits, we have every reason to be vitally concerned about optimum health.

At the very least, your body is the vessel that carries much of what is you. You wouldn't be contented driving an old automobile that burns oil, is difficult to start, and is on the brink of collapse. You probably carefully maintain your car and trade it in when necessary. But are you as meticulous in maintaining that other vehicle that you cannot trade in, your body? Every car comes with an owner's manual. Unfortunately your body, a much more complex and valuable possession, doesn't come with a maintenance schedule and procedures for proper use. So let's go over some health principles and a maintenance plan.

Health Principle One

In America, we have the bad habit of waiting until we're sick before paying attention to our health. In fact, most health insurance plans (until recently) would not pay for regular checkups and consultations if symptoms of disease were not present. This practice has been isolated as one of the major causes of escalating health care costs. The expense is far less when we spend a small amount regularly keeping people healthy rather than spending astronomical amounts for surgery and hospital care after health has deteriorated due to neglect. If this is true on the macrocosmic level of national health care, it is especially accurate on the microcosmic level of the individual's health (you know, an ounce of prevention...) We have abdicated personal responsibility to take care of our health and have placed the responsibility on the health care industry, doctors, and hospitals. We have been reactive, reacting to symptoms of disease and then going to doctors for symptom relief.

We can become proactive about our own health. Proaction means positive action. Rather than waiting for symptoms and then seeking medical attention, we take steps to promote health and fitness. As proactive people, we have responsibilities in every area of life, including health. It's up to us to find out what we need to do to insure physical well-being. We are primarily responsible for our own health. When we have symptoms of dis-ease (the literal meaning of disease), rather than leaving it to the doctor to "make us better," we accept more of the responsibility to improve our health. Being proactive—demonstrating responsibility—

> **TRANSFORMATION:**
>
> *Become proactive about health and put the emphasis upon prevention rather than the care of sickness.*
>
> "A happy heart makes the face cheerful, but heartache crushes the spirit." (Proverbs 15:13)

rather than being reactive—denying responsibility—has a profound effect on our health.

Taking the time to find out what you should be doing and then resolving to follow through with action is what fitness is about. In most cases, some minor changes in our eating and recreation habits will insure physical well-being. It's much easier to stay healthy than it is to recover from illness.

Health Checklists

The Human Population Laboratory of Public Health in Berkeley, California, as early as 1972 found that these seven habits are associated with longevity and good health:

(1) Never smoking cigarettes

(2) Exercising regularly

(3) Maintaining proper weight

(4) Eating breakfast

(5) Not eating unnecessarily between meals

(6) Drinking moderate amounts or no alcohol

(7) Getting seven to eight hours of sleep per night

That's not a difficult list, is it? Good health, when reduced to seven simple habits, is not such a formidable task. It merely takes an initial effort to form the habits and to resist backsliding from your resolve. Research shows that the reward is an average life-span of approximately eleven years longer (if you follow all seven suggestions) than the life- of someone who follows only three or fewer of these habits. However, that's only a small part of the reward. Less sickness, fewer limitations on activity, greater well-being, and more energy go with being proactive about health.

Once you have mastered these seven habits or feel comfortable working within these parameters, this longer list of twenty-one factors for a healthy life is suggested by *Prevention Index*, Rodale Press. According to a survey of experts, these twenty-one factors are ranked in order of their importance in promoting better health:

(1) Not smoking

(2) Not smoking in bed, if you do smoke

(3) Wearing your seat belt

(4) Not drinking and driving

(5) Having a smoke detector in your home

(6) Socializing regularly

(7) Getting frequent strenuous exercise

(8) Drinking alcohol moderately

(9) Avoiding home accidents

(10) Limiting fat in your diet

(11) Maintaining your proper weight

(12) Obeying the speed limit

(13) Getting an annual blood pressure test

(14) Controlling stress

(15) Consuming fiber

(16) Limiting cholesterol in your diet

(17) Getting adequate vitamins and minerals

(18) Having an annual dental exam

(19) Limiting sodium in your diet

(20) Limiting consumption of sugar and sweets

(21) Getting seven to eight hours sleep each night

I was struck by the fact that some of the items on the list are not normally thought of as health-related, such as putting a smoke detector in your home and obeying speed laws, but they do go along with being proactive about your health. This list underscores the fact that health has to do with lifestyle. These are all actions you can take now to avoid sickness. By observing such rules, you are practicing healthy living and taking responsibility for maintaining your own good health.

The American Council on Science and Health adds several other keys to good health not mentioned on the above list but dictated by our changing culture:

♦ Avoid excess sun exposure (use sunscreens)

♦ Practice safe sex

♦ Don't use drugs

Most of the things mentioned here are common sense, and you are probably already observing them. If so, you have already begun to take responsibility for your well-being. You may not be able to immediately observe all the tenets of good health listed here, but at least you can work on the list, congratulating yourself on the steps you have taken. Then you can work one by one on those habits you don't have, attempting those first that are most easily changed or those that have the most direct affect on your health, and then on the other risk factors in turn. You are taking responsibility, and that's what counts!

I can testify to the transformation in energy and well-being that happens when you make the decision to take charge. After I began exercising and only partially watched the food I ate, I almost immediately noticed a difference. I didn't feel the need to sleep after lunch; late afternoon was not a drudgery to get through. I had more energy to do the things I really wanted to do. After only a few weeks of this new regimen, I experienced a newfound energy and enjoyment in living. I realized I couldn't go back to my old habits. I was hooked on this new lifestyle. The benefits far outweighed the effort. Now when I see others at the office struggling to keep from yawning late in the afternoon, I'm thankful for my lifestyle. Whenever I notice others having frequent colds or bouts with the flu that I just seem to avoid, I realize the benefits of health conscious living are innumerable.

Exercising Your Choice

I had tried for years to begin (and continue) an exercise program but always gave it up in frustration persuaded by sore muscles and the agony I felt at the thought of the strenuous effort I'd have to endure. I would put off exercising one more day and, of course, by then the enthusiasm had worn off. I'd find excuses to avoid continuing the exercise program. Then a year later I'd exclaim, "I must do something!" and I'd start the process of enthusiasm, initial soreness, and combined pain, followed by agony, excuses, and loss of motivation once again.

Then I read a simple suggestion that changed this predictable procession toward failure. Like so many good ideas, it was simple and just common sense. I felt I should have known this all along. The suggestion was to start out slowly with any new physical fitness program. You must stop *before* the point of exhaustion. I had always reasoned that since any benefit from walking or running could be felt only if I walked or ran two miles or more, I would have to force myself to endure the pain in reaching this distance as soon as possible. I never could quite stick with it long enough, though. But after finding this tip, I forced myself to start slowly, running just one block, not one mile at a time. Almost as a revelation, I saw I could substitute patience for will power to accomplish the same end result. Rather than rely on will power for endurance, I was patient and started out slowly and easily. "I'll be patient," I told myself, "and in a few weeks I'll work up to a level of endurance that will begin to benefit me."

I jogged just one block. At the end of that block, I was a little winded and could easily have gone further, but I forced myself to stop. The next day I found I wasn't sore; I didn't have to fight the resistance to anticipated pain and drudgery. As a result, I had no problem jogging again for a block. I merely had to remind myself to be patient. I have to admit that my greatest difficulty was the temptation not to admit honestly I was jogging only one or two blocks when I'd relate to someone that I had started a new exercise program.

Within several weeks, I was up to running a half mile and shortly thereafter, a mile. It was accomplished without pain, without sore muscles, without forcing myself to endure agony the next day. It was easy. I just had to be patient. Within three weeks I had formed a new habit, and in a month I admitted, "You know, I really look forward to exercising now since I feel so awake and full of energy when I'm finished!" It didn't take long to build up my endurance so I was able to survive a two- or three-mile run (or walk) without extreme agony.

Another secret is to pick the most convenient time of the day (for me, it's first thing in the morning), stick with that one time, and be patient as you slowly work up to your goal. Once you begin to feel the benefits, it's not difficult to continue. If you haven't already enjoyed the benefits of a regular exercise program, start now, slowly, moderately, without fighting the natural tendency to avoid pain or discomfort. When starting an exercise program, substitute patience for endurance.

A Second Principle

After agreeing to take responsibility, you're now ready for the second major shift in thinking that modern health-consciousness dictates: *Learn to listen to your body!*

You have a unique body. Due to your build and genetic inheritance, you have unique needs. Learn to be conscious of your body telling you what it needs. The big shift in thinking comes in realizing that pain can be good and can be welcomed. Pain tells you something is wrong. It's a warning signal. *Pain can be positive.* It's a help to us. This may be difficult to accept, but look at it this way: If you didn't have nerve receptors that transmit pain in your fingers, and you happened to place your hand on a hot stove, what would happen? You might just keep it there till you were burned severely and incapable of using those fingers until they healed. Pain alerts you to the dangers of continuing to do something detrimental to your health, something you may not have realized is dysfunctional. Pain can be considered the body's built-in alarm system that notifies you of impending danger and that serious consequences are imminent unless you make changes.

Health-consciousness dictates we go to the doctor not with the motive of reducing pain and discomfort but of finding out what we are doing or not doing to maintain health. Often we beg for pills to eliminate the pain and go on our merry way only to find that sometime in the future our bad habits, or lack of consistent good habits, have done serious damage to our bodies. The serious damage may call for major lifestyle alterations or complicated surgical procedures. How much better to do what our bodies dictate before problems become complex and drastic measures are needed!

A corollary of the mindset is the value of preventive medicine. One of the root causes of America's high cost of health insurance is the emphasis placed on treating serious problems without and ignoring the less expensive alternative of taking precautions. The emphasis is on remedy rather than initial prevention. We can make the necessary shifts without having to wait for the medical bureaucracy to take years to make the inevitable shift to the more efficient and natural approach.

When I found that I was having dull headaches in the morning, my initial reaction could have been to take a pain reliever. The fitness alternative was to admit there must be an underlying reason for the pain. My body was telling me (by means of the pain) that my constitution required the elimination of something or the addition of something lacking. Only after medical testing did I learn I had hypoglycemia (low blood sugar). My system does not regulate blood sugar or use it as efficiently as another person's might. To treat the initial problem, I was advised to have light snacks between meals on a regular basis.

Listening to my body and experimenting, I now know exactly when to snack and which snacks are best for me. For instance, I found that a piece of fruit is not as satisfying to me in the morning as it is in the afternoon. My body has told me I need more protein and complex carbohydrates in the mornings. As a result of listening to my body, I again have increased energy and can more readily initiate the enthusiasm to tackle difficult tasks. Moreover,

I have been told that by treating this relatively minor problem now (not with medication but by a change in lifestyle) I have minimized the possibility of having to deal with diabetes, a more serious illness, in the future.

> **TRANSFORMATION:**
>
> *Listen to the body, since pain or disease is the body's way of saying that corrective action needs to be taken to insure continual health.*

Look at pain as a positive help. Don't just seek to eliminate pain, but seek to eliminate the root cause of that pain. Don't mask a problem with medication as a long-term solution, but look for and adopt the necessary lifestyle changes that your body is asking you to make. I am not advocating circumventing of the medical system. I am suggesting only that you not wait for serious problems before finding a physician or health counselor who can offer assistance in taking preventive action through lifestyle changes as the initial solution to a health problem.

A Third Principle

The dynamic mind-body connection known to the ancients and practiced by more nature-conscious cultures to this day is now being verified by medical research. Much scientific research has centered on the relationship between the mind and the immune system in an attempt to explain the mind-body connection. A plethora of studies suggests the beneficial effects on the immune system of positive emotions, such as joy, and love, and optimistic thinking patterns. A study was begun in 1937 with Harvard graduates. Periodic questionnaires were sent over the years to track these men. Researchers discovered that those who were pessimistic in their youth suffered more severe illnesses as they reached their forties, fifties, and sixties, than did the others (Steven Locke, M.D. in *Longevity* 11-88, OMNI International Publishers).

Similarly, a study of the University of Pittsburgh Cancer Institute following the progress of thirty-six breast cancer patients found that a major predictor of survival was the level of happiness and joy. The higher the level of these positive emotions as indicated by standard psychological questionnaires, the greater the chance of survival (David Goleman in *New York Times Magazine*, Sept. 22, 1987, copyright New York Times Co.).

All this is in line with studies conducted over the years that show that socially active, married people live longer than less active single people. In a ten-year study of 2,754 people in Michigan, sociologist James House reports that happily married people live longer than those without a close social network.

Other studies have shown that the brain and immune system are linked by chemicals whose production is stimulated by impulses from the brain (*The Healer Within: The New Medicine of Mind and Body* by Steven Locke, M.D. and Douglas Colligin, published by E.P. Dutton, N.Y.). What all these studies are leading us to consider is that we can use our minds to improve our health. Anyone can take an active part in overcoming illnesses and insuring optimal health. There are techniques that we can learn that augment the healing process. Biofeed-back, coping techniques, and mental reinterpretation of hospital experiences with an emphasis on the positive aspects of the experience are examples of the techniques that can be learned to aid in the healing process. Studies have shown that merely imagining the work your immune system must do to conquer an illness can help the immune system to work more efficiently.

All this research shows that we don't have to accept an illness without our fight-

---

TRANSFORMATION:

Our mental and psychological health has a profound effect on our physical health.

"And the peace of God, which transcends all understanding will guard your hearts and your minds in Christ Jesus." Phil.4:7)

ing back. We don't have to resign ourselves to sentences of hopelessness. Hope is a powerful tool that can be engaged to fight disease. When we acknowledge that we can do something to fight back against illness, the fight is a basis for hope. Also, when the patient has hope, he or she is motivated to seek out techniques for speeding the healing process or at least improving the chances of cure by mentally creating an optimal environment for healing to take place. Thus, the patient takes an active role in both the healing of an illness and the prevention of disease through a healthy mental outlook.

Prevention through mental conditioning is related to the concept of taking a proactive stance in promoting health and accepting personal responsibility for physical health. Fitness and freedom from disease are results of an attitude toward living that can be learned. Realizing that negative or hostile attitudes are associated with an elevated mortality rate, as numerous studies have shown, should motivate us to eliminate cynicism and mistrust. We can work to cultivate an attitude of caring about the welfare of both ourselves and others. We can recognize that there is a relationship between emotions and the body and create an environment that will enhance positive emotions such as love, excitement, and joy in life.

I have a friend, a very successful businessman, who had a heart attack several years ago. He was forced, out of necessity, to rethink his outlook on physical health. He confided that only when he lost his physical health did he realize what a marvelous blessing it was. His misfortune forced him to put more emphasis on what he belatedly realized was most dear to him.

Fortunately, it was not too late. He has since put as much effort into making his physical lifestyle as successful as his career has been. He now carefully watches his food intake, schedules daily exercise, and practices stress reduction techniques. He feels better now than he had for years before his heart attack. Don't wait till you are forced to reconsider your priorities!

Stress

Another aspect of the mind-body relationship is stress and techniques for stress reduction. The pioneer in the study of stress was Hans Selye. In *Stress Without Distress*, he originally described stress as the "non-specific response of the body to any demand made upon it." Selye demonstrated that any agent acting upon a body, whether it be heat, contact with a physical object, or even psychological pain, while having an effect on a specific part of the body, will also force the whole body to adapt to the situation. This non-specific effect on the body to adapt is stress. Both pleasant and unpleasant experiences affect the body. Both demand that the body readjust itself to the situation. Furthermore, the intensity of the stimulus determines the effect that the resultant stress or adaptation pressure will have on the body. Excess stress has a debilitating effect on the body.

Stress is the physical and psychological distress we experience when our day-to-day problems seem to exceed our ability to solve them. A major contribution of science and another breakthrough in health-consciousness is the understanding that stress causes dramatic physiological changes. Stress has such physiological effects as deactivating the immune system, escalating the body's adrenaline production, and speeding up the heartbeat. If prolonged, stress has an enervating effect on the body. Our task is to limit this unnecessary stress.

Selye's recipe for stress reduction twenty years ago is relevant today. To limit the negative effects of stress

> **TRANSFORMATION:**
>
> *Our own mental perspective of events will be manifested in physical effects in our bodies.*

on the body, we must seek our own stress level. Selye said that there are two main types of humans: "The race horses" that thrive on a fast-paced life and "the turtles" who require a tranquil environment. Knowing ourselves and living accordingly are steps toward limiting the negative effects of stress. Similarly, we can choose goals that are really our own rather than goals imposed on us by others.

I like to think of stress in relation to the strings on a violin. Strung too tightly, they might break. But if they're not tight enough, the music is not pleasing. To limit stress requires an assessment of our lives. There are three kinds of activities in life—those things we enjoy doing, those things that are important and should be done, and those things we would not do at all if given a choice. Since we *do* have choices, seek to eliminate that third category of activities! Start focusing on the activities that are important and also pleasing.

Trying to cram too many activities into each day results in an overload and a tearing down of both health and vitality. An example of this is what I call the "materialism merry-go-round." Though there is nothing wrong with material possessions, we need to ask ourselves if we truly require them. First, there is the time spent in working for and then shopping for the latest electronic device. Next, there is the time required to assemble it, learn to use it, maintain and repair it, and finally, the anxiety that comes from realizing we don't use it enough to justify the time and energy we've put into it. It's easy to clutter life and not have the energy left for what is important. We then experience the anxiety that comes with realizing we're not enjoying our lives.

Prescription for Stress Control

Recognize which events in life are stressful. We've all seen the stress rating scales that list stressful events in life and the level of stress each causes. Many events that are intended to be positive are nonetheless stressful. Events such as marriage, a change of jobs, the purchasing of a new home with its new mortgage, a promotion at work—any changes in regular activities are stressful events. The trick is to be aware of the number of stressful events taking place in our lives at any one time. Identify which events are under our own control and which are not. Then it's time to organize, manage, or eliminate the events we *can* control, and perhaps postpone some of these events if we are being inundated by other stressful situations that we *can't* control, such as illness, death of a loved one, or marital difficulties.

The second step is to focus on what's most important—to eliminate spending time and energy on unnecessary, disagreeable activities. Then eliminate guilt by confessing and repenting past sins. Acknowledge mistakes to people you've wronged, make restitution when it's called for, and then move on.

Finally, it's essential to learn to relax. There are many good methods and guides to relaxation techniques. *The Relaxation Response* by Herbert Benson and *Full Catastrophe Living* by Jon Kabat-Zinn have many good suggestions. Following the simple steps outlined here is certain to eliminate a great deal of stress and the enervating effect stress can have on health. Some positive results of stress reduction techniques are elimination of back pain, headache, nausea, and memory problems.

Activity—Medical Check-up

Studies have found two of the most accurate predictors of avoiding heart disease, the number one killer, are lifestyle components. These two predictors are liking your job and your own assessment of your level of happiness. The themes running through health research are (1) lifestyle responsibility and (2) the mind-body connection. The first and most incisive medical check-up is a simple self-examination that does not have to be done at a doctor's office but can be performed simply by asking these three questions. Take the time to do this now, before reading further:

(1) Am I contented?

(2) Do I love my work?

(3) Do I give and receive love regularly?

The answers to these three questions will indicate propensity to longevity far more accurately than cholesterol level or psychological quantitative testing. Once you have completed this check-up, take note of any no answers. Immediately resolve to do something about these detractions from good health. You will find one or more chapters here that can help you. The chapters on Balance and Dreams will show you what you need for contentment. The chapter on Careers will show you how to transform your job into something you love. Finally, the chapters on Legacy and Networking will help bring more love into your life.

Summary

Good health is a lifestyle consideration. Determine if your lifestyle is compatible with health and make the necessary changes. Consider this: At the beginning of the century, the majority of deaths were due to infectious disease. Presently, the vast majority of deaths are due to chronic degenerative diseases, such as cancer, heart attacks, and strokes (arteriosclerosis). These are diseases that can't be controlled by public health measures as can infectious diseases. The major killers of today are diseases of lifestyle and diseases of personal responsibility. Even the latest killer making the headlines, AIDS, though not yet causing anywhere near the deaths attributable to the other major killers, can, in most cases, be considered a disease of lifestyle. The scourge of these illnesses can't be broken by public decree and passive immunization. The prevention is personal responsibility and often a conscious decision to live a lifestyle compatible with healthy and vibrant living.

> **TRANSFORMATION:**
>
> *Physical health is a matter of a healthy lifestyle.*
>
> "Does not wisdom call out? Blessed is the man who listens to me…For whoever finds me finds life and receives favor from the Lord." (Proverbs 8:1, 34, 35)

You can't turn your body in for a newer model. But don't be discouraged. I have a friend who has a fifteen-year-old automobile driven 150,000 miles. It starts up and runs more reliably then many late model cars. There are few reasons why you can't recondition your body to run as efficiently and reliably as any prideful owner of a classic auto has done. Though you can't trade in yours for a new model, you can keep it running in top condition. In fact, a 1965 Mustang or a 1955 Chevy Belair is more exciting to me to watch rolling down the road than a brand new late model BMW, anyway!

Initiate an attitude of health-consciousness by monitoring your health and looking for ideas and suggestions that will help you to live a healthy lifestyle.

Wellness is a way of life. It's a regular, systematic way of living in which you accept your responsibility to be accountable for your own well-being.

"A wise man should consider that health is the greatest of human blessings, and learn how by his own thought to derive benefit from his illness." (Hippocrates)

"Good health to you." (Acts 15:29, NW Translation)

CHAPTER 5

Acquiring Allegiance (Faith)

As I look back on my life, one factor stands out in accounting for my contentment and relative success. Over the years, my conception of a higher power has evolved, but the overarching principle has remained. I have always had an inherent optimism based firmly on the belief that life came about for a reason and that it is going somewhere. Life has a direction, and since I'm part of life, my life must have some direction to it, too. That simple belief has given me the optimism to see past emergencies and exigencies, to suspend judgment about a disconcerting event until the difficulty plays itself out.

Meaning to life is one of the central issues we must confront. One of the recurring themes of this book is that what we think, our perceptions of ourselves and the world around us, affects our actions. I can think of no more pervasive issues in life than *Why am I here?* and *Where is my life going?* Is there any doubt that how we answer these questions can have a profound effect on what we do with our lives? I have some ideas that may help one find satisfactory answers.

This chapter is not intended to be a complete guide to faith. Nor does it propose to answer most questions about faith, or even to point one in a definite direction in the search for spiritual enlightenment. This subject is far too personal for that. Furthermore, I can't adequately cover a subject beyond the physical using only physical language and physical terms. What I will do is this:

♦ Help you better understand what spirituality is and is not

♦ Suggest why you should open yourself to this life aspect

♦ Offer several options for starting your personal search

I am a Christian. I have found my relationship with God in Christ (the Father, Son, and Holy Spirit) to be the most fulfilling and exciting aspect of my life. I acknowledge that only through them have I attained value in my life. What a glorious sensation to know I can turn to someone with far greater wisdom than I for guidance and to know He cares for me as I would expect a perfect father would! As Scripture says, "Blessed is the man that trusts in you." (Psalm 84:12) However, I'm not going to talk about theology. I will talk to you as if you had no understanding of or experience with a higher power. If this is your situation, I hope you will consider my reasoning on why you must take up a search for a spiritual experience in your life. If you already have a faith, I intend this will help reaffirm your faith and give you ideas on how you can approach others in a non-threatening and logical way with evidence that a spiritual outlook is critical for your total success in living.

Throughout history, people have found personal meaning and solid foundations for their lives through religious faith. But faith in religious institutions has been severely shaken in the past thirty to forty years. Religion, in general, has a different position in society than it once had. Statistics show, for example, that though there has been a decrease in religious affiliation in recent years, there has been an increase in belief in mysticism. Similarly, while a number of people consider themselves less religious, they rate themselves as more spiritual. What these statistics show is a shift in perception of faith and spirituality. For some, faith and spirituality are less thought of in religious terms but more in philosophical terms. Nonetheless, the increase in spiritual appreciation, along with the consistent number of people believing in God (93 percent in the U.S.), reveals a groping for spiritual affiliation and understanding. Do you share society's ambivalence? Are you settled in what you believe and why?

Faith or spirituality is a central issue in life and needs to be addressed. If you ask and attempt to answer the questions, *Why am I here?* or *What is life about?* or *What meaning does life have to me?*, the results are profound. You begin to see beyond the material, and you begin to add a new dimension to your life. The beginning of spirituality is the quest for meaning in life! Whether you have faith in a higher power or faith in yourself or even in the human race, it's still faith. Even if you say, "I don't know what I have faith in," you are still living as if to say, "I have faith that my noncommitment to anything is the best course for me at the moment." However, I submit it is better to confront these issues and make conscious decisions rather than to abdicate your power over these decisions. I also assert that this issue of spirituality affects all other areas of life—family, friends, career, physical well-being, and others.

A life that is completely self-centered loses its excitement over time. Searching for physical success, for example, has its limitations. After a while, material possessions and the trappings of success don't quite carry the satisfaction they once did. If you do not expand your horizon, your life can quickly become dull and uninteresting. A spiritual outlook will assure you that you won't lose your enjoyment in living.

What Does It Mean?

When we speak of spirituality, what do we mean? Religiosity and spirituality can be as different as a beam of light is from a physical structure. If you're not aware, you can walk right through a light beam without even noticing it. You can't ignore a physical structure like a building, though. Religiosity is like a physical structure that can be easily described and conveyed by written rules and set customs. Spirituality is not so easily conveyed. It's a way of being, a way of thinking. How do you describe the consistency of a ray of light? However, as different as the two are, they both can lead to faith.

The Bible speaks of faith this way: "And what is faith? Faith gives substance to our hope and makes us certain of realities we do not see." (Hebrews 11:1, New English Bible) A formal approach through religion or an informal approach for finding meaning (spirituality) can each lead to the same concept, faith—the assurance and certainty that life has inherent meaning.

Spirituality has everything to do with one's meaning for existence. It defines our place in the order of things, our place in society, in the world, and in the universe. In fact all spiritual questing, whether it be from a mystical orientation or a purely humanistic orientation (devoid of divinity) is centered around uncovering the answers to several important questions: *Who am I? How should I live? What is the meaning of my life?* These are important questions, and the way you answer them definitely has an effect on your life, even if you answer with the statement, "I don't care." A spiritual person is one who courageously seeks to find answers to these questions.

Spirituality is a quest for a place in the universe, the search for a connection to the world. This feeling of connection to the universe is the essence of spirituality. It includes a communion with God, with others, and with nature. As you wake up spiritually, you realize that you are part of the universe. I use the word *universe* here because I don't want to limit the reader's thinking to the world around him, only. How far one's awareness and influence extend is a personal issue for each of us to decide.

We all have a natural reverence for living things. We care about others, for example. When we care about others we recognize our affinity to all other living things. We realize there is something greater than ourselves. What this *something greater* is, whether we define that as God, or as nature, or as the universe, we realize we are part of something vaster than ourselves, something that transcends us. Once we realize that there is something greater than ourselves, we begin walking on the path of spirituality. Over time, our understanding of that greater power will undoubtedly broaden and may even change, but we begin to sense a purpose for life. Life is no longer empty; it begins to take on meaning—and what a profound change this brings!

Reverence for life may take the form of reverence for and desire to serve God or may start out as simply a reverence for nature and a desire to preserve the ecology. I have always felt an immediate communion or attachment to any person who has either orientation, one toward nature or toward God. I feel the two are related. Regardless, the hallmark of spirituality is a linkage to the universe that includes your *role, goal* and *soul.* This connection is a feeling that exceeds description. I know of no greater feeling than that of being settled and content, knowing a course that gives true meaning and fulfillment. This is the gift of spirituality.

TRANSFORMATION:

Spirituality includes a recognition of our connection to the world around us and to something greater than ourselves.

"The Spirit himself testifies with our spirit that we are God's children." (Romans 8:16)

I have a friend named Alice who rejected her family's religious upbringing in the seventies when she was a teenager. At the time, she didn't feel the experience was relevant to her life. Only later, when she married and had children, was she faced with life's difficult questions which called on faith for answers. What was she going to tell her children? Only then did she begin her personal search. She was motivated to find answers. She asked others; she read; she meditated. Only after coming to conclusions with which she felt satisfied, did she feel competent to help her children gain a firm footing in their lives. And only after coming to conclusions that were relevant to her, did Alice begin looking again for a place of worship. She reasoned that the structure of religion would help her to convey certain guiding principles of life to her children. In Alice's case, religion was her means of passing on to her family the spirituality she had found for herself.

Starting on the Path

I've talked to many people who have felt something was missing from their lives, a spiritual gap that needed to be filled. Some speak of it as a growing dissatisfaction with answers provided by materialism and scientific progress. Evidence is everywhere that there is a search for answers that speak to the spirit. New Age mysticism has gained influence even among intellectuals who once were staunchly secular. The reason for this, I think, is the craving people have for spirituality that has not been satisfied by churches that spend their time on social issues rather than first satisfying the hunger for spiritual guidance. Even the field of psychology, an area that has traditionally eschewed spiritual explanation, has seen the loss of favor with Freudian psychology and a popularity of Jungian psychology, which teaches that in each of us there is an innate drive toward self-awareness and a need to connect with something larger than ourselves. Jungian psychology also teaches that there is a *collective unconscious* rooted in instincts. In fact, a growing number of therapists are encouraging their patients to seek the guidance of church or temple in conjunction with their regular visits to a therapist. Many therapists also recognize the success of dependency treatment groups, such as Alcoholics Anonymous, which assert the existence of a "higher power" and the need people for help from that "higher power." Indeed, most therapists can see the relevance of seeking for and maintaining a sense of purpose in life.

The one thing that all of these approaches, including traditional Christianity, current psychology, New Age movement, and other spiritual approaches, have in common is the human desire to have a purpose in life. No one has enumerated that need more eloquently than Victor Frankel in his classic, *Man's Search for Meaning*. Frankel, a psychologist, was himself a victim of German concentration camps in World War II. He experienced in his own life and observed in others the power of the meaning in life. He concluded that one of the main determinants of survival under those extremely torturous conditions was an overriding sense of purpose in life. Those having a purpose in life, a goal to accomplish some deed, whether it be magnanimous or rooted in revenge, were far more apt to survive the perils of camp life. After he was released from captivity, he continued his study of meaning in life and reported a high success rate in his psychiatric practice among patients who successfully found an individual purpose in life.

No one can provide that purpose in life for another. Only by seeking and meditating does this reason for living emerge. The successes reported in the chapter on goal-setting are testimonies to the power inherent in a clear direction and purpose for life. However, self-gratification is not an adequate purpose in life. Only a cause larger than oneself will serve us and lead us to believe that life is worth living.

What Spirituality Is

In summary, spirituality is related to these life attitudes:

(1) Recognition that we are linked to all other life, past, present and future

(2) Desire to seek our personal purpose for living

(3) Reverence for nature

(4) Acceptance that there are forces or powers not perceptible to our traditional physical senses

(5) Acceptance that life can and does have meaning

The first step is to simply begin seeking. It's that simple! As we spend time alone listing the values we feel are important, we begin to clarify our purpose.

List on paper the qualities, abilities, or traits you feel are most important. First list qualities, such as love, justice, honesty, responsibility, kindness, etc. When you put these in order of importance, you get a sense of what is most important. You may be surprised to realize what things actually hold the most meaning. Surveys I've done of students, both younger and older, consistently reveal that family and a sense of belonging are very high on the list. Once you isolate the qualities and possessions most important to you and then make time for those needs, you begin to experience contentment and fulfillment. This search for meaning is on-going—fortunately, since this never-ending quest keeps life exciting. Over time your search yields clearer pictures of what you feel you are here to accomplish.

Do this:

(1) List the values, possessions, abilities, and experiences most important to you.

(2) Put these in order according to levels of priority.

(3) Decide which of these priorities are unfulfilled.

(4) Schedule time to pursue those priorities.

(5) Always be open to experiences and insights that will help clarify your values.

(6) Expand your horizons beyond yourself and seek a purpose bigger than yourself.

(7) Expect to continue growing in your understanding of life.

Mind-Body Connections

I've presented reasoning, evidence, and ideas to show you the need to open yourself to spiritual experiences. As long as you are open to such experiences, you will be led in the direction best for you. Once you set a goal, your mind automatically works as a *homing* device and becomes attuned to information that will be useful to your chosen course. This is especially true with spiritual experiences. Once you recognize your need to be more fully connected to the universe and you see the need to have goals greater than yourself, your attention will be opened to opportunities for spiritual growth. It's beyond the scope of this book to endorse any one avenue or approach. This is not to say that all paths are acceptable; I don't feel they are. However, I don't want you to lose touch with the

> **TRANSFORMATION:**
>
> *Begin a quest to find your personal meaning in life and continually seek to refine that meaning.*
>
> "Seek first his kingdom and his righteousness, and all these things will be given to you as well." (Matthew 6:33)

important insight that spiritual growth is necessary for your personal growth by generating debate on which course is the correct one.

Spirituality means connection to the universe and connection, recognition, or communion with something greater than and beyond yourself. I'll leave it up to the reader to define what *universe* and *something greater* means, whether those terms mean a personal God, or a force greater than oneself. Spiritual matters, by definition, go beyond the mind. To insist that everyone understand this higher power in my highly personal terms only would be arrogant. Seek that which will complete your understanding of life and that something that is beyond your physical senses.

In *Relaxation Response*, Herbert Benson has chronicled experiments that cite prayer as an aid toward physical health and the connection between mind and body. Benson did his first experiment with Transcendental Meditation (TM). He and fellow researcher, Robert Keith Wallace, found that repeated mantras replaced the excited thoughts that kept a person tense during the day. By following a system of meditation, devotees are able to lower metabolic rate, slow down heart rate, and lower blood pressure. Other experiments along these lines are delineated in Chapter 4 on "Body Basics." Benson also found that the same results are confirmed when devotees of all major religious traditions repeat their simple repetitious prayers. Each method created what he called the *relaxation response*. Since then, Benson has found that people who used actual prayers, rather than trite or meaningless phrases, had improved results with stress relief and actual healing of the body. Benson dubbed this phenomenon *the faith factor*.

Work at the Mind/Body Institute at New England Deaconess Hospital in Boston has reported convincing evidence that people who feel in touch with God are less likely to get sick and have fewer stress-related symptoms. Subjects of the experiments themselves concluded that prayer strengthened their spirits and healed the body.

Experimentation with prayer continues. In March 1996, *Reader's Digest* published an article entitled "Does Prayer Heal?"

A study in 1988 of 393 heart patients at San Francisco General Medical Center Hospital confirmed that patients who were prayed for by people they had never met or with whom they had had no contact had a better recovery rate than patients for whom there was not an organized prayer. The doctors conducting these experiments were very careful to follow the established rules of scientific research—patients were randomly selected and divided into two groups, the experimental and the control group, and neither the patients nor the doctors or nurses knew which patients were being prayed for by volunteers. Statistically, the results were beyond coincidence. *Prayer does heal.* Researchers had to admit that something was happening that the physical laws of science could not explain. This is *the faith factor* and an indication that spiritual aspects of life cannot be ignored. Without physical contact or the knowledge they were being prayed for, patients were affected by the prayers of others. This is termed *non-localized prayer* and to date there is no other explanation except faith and spirituality.

The majority of the 52 percent of people in America who report praying at least once a day (National Opinions Research Center, 1991) feel that their prayers are often answered though perhaps not in the way they originally envisioned. A study published by sociologist Margaret M. Poloma in conjunction with George H. Gallup, Jr. entitled, "Varieties of Prayer," reports that prayer helps people to experience inner peace and a feeling of "divine intimacy" or "being led by God." At times, prayer is the only avenue some feel

---

TRANSFORMATION:

There are metaphysical forces at work in the universe available to us individually that cannot be understood by the current laws of physics.

"The Spirit helps us in our weakness. We do not know what we ought to pray for, but the Spirit himself intercedes for us with groans that words cannot express." (Romans 8:26)

is available to them for experiencing unconditional love. By praying and then listening in silence, those interviewed said they experienced the "presence of God."

As substantiated reports of results come in, more psychologists are praying with and prescribing prayer for their patients. Diverse practitioners, such as those at the Samaritan Institute of Denver, Yale-trained psychiatrist George Hogben, M.D. in New York, and psychologist Joan Borgsenko, Ph.D. of the Mind/Body Health Institute in Massachusetts have reported excellent results with prayer. Although the forces involved can't be explained, it is not necessary that we fully understand the forces at work in order to employ them for personal growth.

A Way of Life

One of the basic questions that a spiritual person needs to answer is, *How should I live?* Even a person with no religious interest must sit up and take note of the fact that practitioners of each of the world's religions have independently come to similar conclusions.

We live in a world guided by hedonism and a cynical philosophy that claims since there are no absolutes, no course of action is better than any other. Still, human life needs some direction. Most religious philosophers and the vast majority of secular philosophers have come to the same conclusion that a virtuous or principled life is the only one worth living.

From purely logical reasoning, Socrates and Plato concluded that it is far more important to live by principle than merely to live. Happiness will never come from merely existing. Only living a life of which we can be proud will bring contentment. If you wish to live a happy and successful life, you must base your life on certain unchanging principles. Build your own list of tenets by which to live. Principles such as courage, loyalty, and wisdom can serve you in your life direction, similar to a compass pointing out physical directions. Science has shown that an organism cannot survive in a chaotic environment. The physical universe has order. I submit that it is necessary to assume the world is built on unchanging principles. By doing so ourselves, we incorporate some constancy and predictability into our lives, something that will enhance our ability to cope. In a world where abundant wealth and perfect health are not guaranteed, here is something that we can count on, something totally under our control—insistence on living a life based on personal and permanent principles.

A doctor I know confided there was a time life ceased to have much meaning for him. Focusing on hospital bureaucracy and endless deadlines led to drudgery, which led to negative thinking and depression. Fortunately, George came to the point of admitting that something was missing from his life. The spark of excitement was gone. He grappled with the negatives of life. As he groped for answers, he made a momentous discovery. He acknowledged that there were no easy answers and sought an explanation on a higher plane, beyond the physical, hence the term *metaphysical* (above the physical). To him that meant not being so quick to dismiss any idea that could not be substantiated by hard facts.

Like George, only by confronting these issues of life beyond pure material evidence will you find quieting, satisfying answers. He found what he needed in the writings of Albert Schweitzer. Schweitzer, the legendary Alsation missionary doctor in Africa and winner of the 1952 Nobel peace prize, had wrestled with the same questions. As a result of his questioning, Schweitzer formulated what became for him a unifying principle of life. This central principle of meaning was succinctly referred to as "reverence for life." He had earlier in his life been a clergyman but came to find that he could do more good as a physical healer than as a spiritual healer. A desire to preserve life became his guiding principle.

George, after a period of meditation, decided to accept this same principle as his own central theme of meaning. Once he had settled on this central principle, he began rebuilding his life upon this sturdy structure. Once he could clearly aver that "preservation of life" was important to him and within his power, he could begin to rearrange his own life accordingly. His solution for discouragement was to spend more time helping others regain their health and less time on paperwork, meetings, and hospital politics. He regained the satisfaction of knowing his own life was making a difference again. George also found a church where he could experience the camaraderie of those who radiated a need to care for others in their own ways as he had come to care for others using his special talents and abilities.

Activity

My wife's experience in accepting her quest to regain a spiritual connection and find new meaning in her life may help you. Marlene had been left confused and deeply hurt by the dogmatic assertions and unbending structure she endured in the church in which she had been raised. Finally, the uncaring, uncompassionate structure was too much to endure, but before giving up the spiritual part of her life, she decided to make one more independent search for spiritual understanding. After praying and asking for guidance, she had the idea of clearing aside all denominational rhetoric and debate over dogma and simply read the words of Jesus in the Bible as if she never had heard of Jesus before. This way, she reasoned, she could listen to the words of the reputed greatest Teacher of all time without bias and preconceived notions. She got a "red letter" edition of the Bible in which Jesus' words are highlighted. Almost immediately after starting to read, she could discern what Christianity was really about, and her spiritual outlook immediately was strengthened.

If you have misgivings about organized religion or are unclear about what spirituality is, try Marlene's idea. Get a "red letter" edition of the Bible and start in the book of Matthew, the first book of the New Testament, and begin reading Jesus' words only. Do it with an open mind. To this day, one third of the world's population is deeply influenced by, though not necessarily living by, his credo. You'll begin to see clearly from the words of the greatest Teacher what spirituality really means and how it can make a difference in your life. What makes his words so inspiring are that they are spoken in clear, everyday language without pomp or pretension.

In Luke 12:22-8, Jesus taught about the power of believing in a Higher Power that could be conceived of as a loving father and friend, a wise father to whom one can confidently come for help and know that he or she would never be rejected:

"Therefore I tell you, do not worry about your life, what you will eat; or about your body, what you will wear. Life is more than food, and the body more than clothes. Consider the raven: They do not sow or reap, they have no storeroom or barn; yet God feeds them. And how much more valuable you are than birds! Who of you by worrying can add a single hour to his life? Since you cannot do this very little thing, why do you worry about the rest?

"Consider how the lilies grow. They do not labor or spin. Yet I tell you, not even Solomon in all his splendor was dressed like one of these. If that is how God clothes the grass of the field, which is here today, and tomorrow is thrown in to the fire, how much more will he clothe you, O you of little faith!"

> **TRANSFORMATION:**
>
> *Live your life in such a way that you are true to the principles that have stood the test of time. Valued spiritual ideas.*

Now continue this activity on your own, reading from the words of Jesus found in the books of Matthew, Mark, Luke, and John of the Bible.

Seeking that connection to something greater than yourself will draw you toward the sublime, to the unchanging principles you seek. Just observing the universally accepted concepts that are timeless and have been taught for thousands of years is a good beginning. Immediately once this resolve to live by timeless, unselfish principles is made, notice how your self-esteem sky-rockets. That experience in itself should assure you that you have taken the course that's right for you.

Valued Spiritual Ideas

Next let's explore four basic spiritual viewpoints worthy of cultivation. These thoughts can be confirmed by numerous independent sources:

The universe is greater than we are.

We are part of something beyond our comprehension and greater than ourselves. This thought can be comforting and reassuring—we are not alone! However, it's also true that we must be humble enough to acknowledge, "I am not all-important! My welfare is not the only viewpoint that needs to be considered. There is something greater at stake." Comforting, also, is realizing that we are part of this something greater, though only a small part.

There is more to the universe than the physical we detect with our senses.

Science reveals gaps in its ability to explain some phenomena. How short-sighted it is to claim, "I can't believe it unless it's proved." Science does not presently have all the tools necessary for proof. Rather than put your life on hold till all the evidence is in, you can believe and dream. That's what faith is—the ability to dream, to believe that things are possible without having the evidence at your fingertips. Faith also helps us believe there are forces beyond those that can be detected by our physical senses. "Now faith is being sure of what we hope for and certain of what we do not see." (Hebrews 11:1) You know this even though you don't have irrefutable proof. There is enough partial evidence, hints around you, so you can accept this as reality. You are not stifled by not being able to explain everything. You need not have all the evidence and explanations before you use the power. Just as mankind has used electricity for years without having a full explanation of it, you, the spiritual person, use unexplained powers that are available without a full comprehension of their mean-

ing. You have the faith that the seemingly impossible is possible
and can come to pass for you.

Life is going somewhere.

There is a direction toward the fulfillment of the universe.
The spiritual person is, therefore, optimistic. This is, in fact, a
corollary of faith. "I can dream that things will get better." The
universe is seeking its fulfillment. Science avers that life is evolving. Science cannot provide evidence as to why this is so or how
it happens, but it does confirm life is indeed evolving and ever-
changing. A spiritual person takes this as a sign that there is direction to the universe. We are going somewhere. There is a purpose.

In spite of the negatives, the spiritual person looks at things
in a positive way. In spite of the four main bases for negativism,
he is positive. These four possible negatives need not make us
negative. Our allegiance to or recognition of a higher force helps
us confront these four possible negatives:

(1) Death—we are finite as far as can be proven; of course, I
hope you believe there is something more.

(2) Loneliness—we are born alone and we die alone, and
these are both actions no one else can do for us.

(3) Responsibilities come with freedom—this can be frightening. There are always choices to make, and it can be
unnerving to think that we can make wrong choices and
that decisions can affect us for years, for life. Even when
we abdicate our freedom, we're still responsible.

(4) Meaning in life—this can be difficult to find. Some feel
they have to grope for some explanation to make sense
out of their existence.

These factors can be frightening and can make us fearful of
taking responsibility for life. The wonderful thing is that the
spiritual person realizes there is inherent meaning in the universe. It may not be clear, it may not be readily apparent, but we
can take solace in knowing it's there. Eventually, we feel certain
we will find it. We are certain, too, that we need never be alone.
We can be in touch with something greater and a part of something greater.

We must take responsibility for living our own lives.

Each of us has something to offer and a part to play in the scheme of things. No one else can do it. The world can be a better place because we have lived. If we don't take the responsibility, the world has lost something of value, and we have lost out on the satisfaction and joy of fulfilling that responsibility. Even if we don't want to accept the responsibility, the consequences are forced on us. We cannot escape.

Allegiance and Its Value

The four principles of spirituality are:

(1) We are part of something greater than ourselves.

(2) Faith in things beyond the physical world is possible.

(3) An optimistic outlook leads to hope.

(4) We are responsible to find our own place.

We, as a spiritual people, have several major advantages in life. Life is not shallow. There is meaning. There is direction. When we have allegiance to a higher power, we have a compass to find the way. Though we may feel at times that we are in the midst of a vast forest unable to see beyond a few trees and unable to see a path, still we have a compass to continually point the general direction. We need not walk in circles.

Kierkegaard, the Danish Christian theologian and philosopher (1813-1855), once said people are like soldiers who come to earth with sealed orders. Our responsibility is to discern what those orders are and to fulfill them. Yes, there can be meaning to life. It is up to us to find that meaning. It may require a lifelong commitment to find and clarify that meaning, stating it in a way that is personally relevant and understandable. The spiritual person is certain eventually to find his or her way. Everyone strives for validation of existence. If we are spiritual, we are certain to attain that validation. There is a quiet confidence that it will begin to make sense even if it does not at the moment.

Since each of us is unique, we may state life's meaning differently from others. Why can't the apprehension of life's meaning be more simple and readily apparent? For some, it may be simple, but others have the habit of making things difficult. Some derive enough meaning in life from the assurance that the universe is going toward a grand fulfillment, or stated another way, God has a magnificent purpose and that we need only contribute something to that grand fulfillment. Meaning may be found in completing some difficult and long-range task. Meaning may be found in feeling we have done something to make the world a better place. Meaning may be found in feeling we have left a legacy of a sort that will survive our tenure here. Meaning may even be found in making a systematic search for understanding and meaning itself. Some may state this meaning simply while others may not rest till the more complex details become apparent.

Just as a film is judged most worthy of watching when the ending is not apparent and a good story is enhanced by not knowing what to expect in the end, the living of our lives is enhanced by not knowing what the ending will be. We might liken our existence to that of actors in a film or play. At this point, we don't know what the ending of our story or humanity's story will be, but that's what makes it so exciting. However, it is enough to be assured the ending will be worth the wait. Faith and optimism lead to believing there will be a happy ending!

TRANSFORMATION:

Life is inexorably moving toward some fulfillment, and the spiritual person wishes to submit rather than resist it.

"The creation waits in eager expectation for the sons of God to be revealed. We know that the whole creation has been groaning as in the pains of childbirth right up to the present time." (Romans 8:19,22)

*"Great men are they who see that the spiritual is stronger than
any material force, that thoughts rule the world."
(Ralph Waldo Emerson)*

*"Store up for yourselves treasures in heaven, where moth
and rust do not destroy, and where thieves do not
break in and steal." (Matthew 6:20)*

CHAPTER 6

Living Legacy
(Family)

Before I could blink, I was twenty-one!—married with a baby on the way. I was going to be a father, responsible for another person, and yet had barely become responsible for myself. The realization was daunting. My strategy for coping was to put it out of mind, thinking, I hope it will all work out. Somehow it did in my case, but, looking back, I would have preferred being spared the worry and frustration of not knowing whether I was making the right decisions. I had one thing going for me, though. As it turned out, it was the most important thing. I had been raised in a stable family which lived by Christian principles. Of course, in our contemporary world many traditions have been questioned and rethought, but the value of a secure upbringing is again conceded to be indispensable.

When I became a father, I just followed the model set by my father, and it wasn't a bad script with which to start. However, as society has changed so drastically, adjustments have had to be made. In my case, I beat the odds. Families with a father at twenty-two and a mother at eighteen don't usually last, but here we are still married many years later with three children of whom we are proud. I was fortunate. Along the way I learned the value of having a close family, having roots and security. I also learned some principles of living that accounted for our success.

Sociologists and psychologists agree that family heritage has a profound effect on people. However, family is a double-edged sword. It can be a help or a hindrance. It can provide the nurturance and support for growth, or it can block further growth. You are affected by others close to you, and you in turn influence how they will act in the world outside the family. Family can be a powerful motivational influence and source of security in your life, regardless of your family position. You deserve an optimum family life, and the acceptance and practice of a few basic principles I'll present here may make all the difference.

For purposes here, by "family," I mean a group of two or more who love and care for each other, since this is the definition preferred by 74 percent of Americans (Massachusetts Mutual Life Survey, 1990).

Family is a source of roots, an ongoing source of socialization and where we learn to function in and view society. Many of the traits, habits, and views we now possess and that we will carry throughout our lives are formulated through family environment. One reason family has such a great influence is the tendency to let down our guard around those familiar to us. As a result, we more readily absorb the ideas, ideals, and habits of those close to us.

Living in a rapidly changing world, what an asset to have a place where we can go as a haven from the problems and difficulties precipitated by change! Robert Frost spoke of the home as "the place where, if you go there, they have to take you in." To have such a place is a stabilizing influence in life, a legacy. I call this chapter "Legacy" since as a family member, you are the legacy of your parents, and as parents, you have a legacy to pass on.

I frequently hear social observers intimating that the family is losing its influence, or that somehow it is becoming anachronistic, or at best, is becoming an optional institution in society. However, whenever I do surveys of personal values, invariably "having a happy family life" is chosen among the top values of importance. These findings are consistent, regardless of economic status, gender, age, education, or other demographics. Respondents to my surveys rate having a happy family a major desire in life. So while some claim family influence may be waning, people fervently desire fulfillment in this area of their lives. Biblically, family is so important that even people who do not have living physical families can still be members of the family of God. "We are God's children; and if children, then heirs. We are God's heirs." (Romans 8:16,17)

The Legacy of Family

Perhaps as the world appears more impersonal, there is more of a craving for a sense of belonging and caring. Even highly successful people lament the gap they feel is left in their lives if they are not members of closely knit families. Unfortunately, social commentators have been ambivalent about the need for strong families. Let me set the record straight: Speaking from my perspective as a sociologist, the family is the most powerful institution we encounter in life. While 55 percent of U.S. households (U.S. Census Bureau, 1993) are headed by married couples, my surveys have found this is the standard the vast majority of respondents wish to emulate, if possible. Although the traditional family is barely in the majority, it is still the standard that most people seek for themselves.

The family is important, since this structure can provide all the basic human needs necessary for a fully functioning individual. These needs are:

(1) *Security*—including physical needs, such as food, shelter, physical affection

(2) *Love*—recognition, belonging, caring

(3) *Structure*—order and the trust that it engenders

(4) *Intellectual growth*—interaction and stimulation

(5) *Self-esteem*—self-worth and personal identity

(6) *Self-actualization*—the development of our unique abilities

(7) *Spirituality*—meaning in life and universal core values

The above checklist is given for two reasons. First, all of those needs listed are provided by a functional family. Though they can be provided in other ways through other sources, family is the only structure in society that can provide *all* of these simultaneously. The recognition of this fact alone demonstrates the potential power for good of a functional family. Commentators and social activists who seek to negate the family system are neglecting the most powerful means we have for promoting human growth and potential. By striving to be part of or establishing a functional family, we not only avail ourselves of potential benefits, but also provide those close to us privileges that are not available to many. Family is a powerful influence. Strive to work for the kind of family arrangement that will be a positive influence in your life, and insure a legacy for the future.

The second reason for the above-mentioned list is to provide a checklist as a suggested set of goals for family. By using this checklist, you can gauge the success of your own family. Unfortunately, some see only the obvious functions of a family and don't recognize the potential that their family could fulfill. Satisfaction of all the above needs can be provided for both children and adults alike through this system. You have some powerful resources available to you. As a family member, you can strive to make this environment the basis of a legacy that will have a tremendous influence on you and those close to you.

We'll examine different aspects of family life, such as mate selection, marriage relations, parenting, and divorce. Some of the valuable lessons that have been verified by research in the last thirty years will be mentioned. I hope you will discover some useful concepts to enhance your family legacy.

The Exchange Theory

One concept frequently alluded to in social psychology is the exchange theory. Much interaction in life is bound up in "exchange." You may be familiar with the concept in business. Business is essentially organized exchange. Goods and services are exchanged for other goods and services or their equivalent. In business, participants expect fairness. They expect something of equal or greater value to what they are offering. If they are offering their services as an employee in exchange for a wage, they expect to be paid what their services are worth. By the same token, the employer has a right to expect service equivalent to the monetary compensation offered. This concept is true with regard to friendship, courtship, and marriage, though not as readily acknowledged. A friendship or any relationship lasts as long as there is an equal exchange or a perceived equal exchange. This is a basic principle of life that's very simple, yet explains far more complex dynamics in society. For example, you will cultivate friendships only as long as you feel you are being treated fairly. You may stay in a relationship due to other factors, but you will only actively cultivate the relationship if you feel you are offered something of value, or something you need, in return. Note how this concept explains relationships, courtships, and eventual marriages. Entering into a relationship, take stock of some of the things of value you may bring into the unconscious yet inevitable exchange:

◆ Physical attractiveness

◆ Education

◆ Emotional support

◆ Love and caring

◆ Intelligence

◆ Status

◆ Masculine/feminine qualities

◆ Well-paying occupation

◆ Ambition

◆ Faithfulness and loyalty

Only a naive person would argue that most of these traits are not in some way taken into account when pursuing a relationship. Exchange explains why a college-educated doctor from the upper class will probably not enter into an enduring relationship with a high-school-educated janitor from the working class unless the janitor has something perceived as valuable by the doctor, such as an extremely physical or emotional attraction. This has little to do with prejudice, but is simply part of an unconscious exchange. The doctor merely wishes to be compensated for her valuable assets in any relationship, whether between friends or with a spouse.

Recognizing this, I'd like to point out two ramifications of this theory-concept that are so simple yet so profound as to explain the success or failure of any relationship, especially marriage. Bear

in mind that this exchange is taking place, albeit subconsciously, as a person seeks a relationship. He will look for assets in another person he considers most valuable, all the time highlighting the traits or qualities he brings to the exchange. Frequently marriages are doomed to failure when partners do not appear to be getting that which they feel they are enti-

> **TRANSFORMATION:**
>
> *A relationship lasts as long as each perceives a fair exchange of values.*
>
> Biblical justice principle:
> "Eye for an eye, tooth for a tooth." (Exodus 21:24)

tled. For example, a man may initially put on a pretense of being caring and thoughtful, then put the pretense aside after marriage. The tentative exchange of equivalence is altered to the extent that the spouse no longer feels she has been treated fairly, and the relationship disintegrates. If you want a long-term relationship, offer only what you are capable of delivering! Offer only what you are willing to continue to deliver. An initial deception will only be the source of future pain.

The second point is that needs and desires change over time. What may have been considered valuable in a relationship at one time may cease to hold the same value or simply be unavailable later. Physical attractiveness may or may not be valued more as time goes on. You can do your part to insure that a relationship remains strong and vital by being sensitive to the changing needs of your spouse. By increasing another behavior or trait of value in place of one that is no longer valued or no longer possible to deliver, the exchange balance is maintained. Many women, for example, have enhanced their value by pursuing a career and well-paying occupation (though this may not have been their original intention when entering marriage).

You may consider this blunt, insensitive counsel, but unfortunately, it's reality. All the complaining and objecting will not negate this principle of life. Far better than fighting against this principle would be to understand and employ it. In many long-lasting relationships, partners are not as physically attractive or energetic as they once were. While physical assets begin to depreciate in value, other characteristics can appreciate to compensate. The caring and sensitivity a couple display toward each other that come with sharing many years and experiences together becomes of great value in the exchange. While the value of physical attractiveness may decline, other qualities can increase in worth. Conscious effort, though, may be required to maintain a fair exchange. You must take the initiative to provide for the needs and wants of others. You take the responsibility to preserve the balance.

Transformation of Marriage

The family has undergone major changes in the last thirty years. These changes can be better understood by accepting that marriage has undergone a transformation from an institution to a relationship. For instance, roles in many families have experienced major changes with traditional standards not as readily accepted without question. Marriage is no longer valued by many as an institution in the sense that an institution in social terms refers to an arrangement of society that is relatively stable from generation to generation. Marriage now offers different expectations. Participants look to marriage as a relationship and a vehicle for self-fulfillment. Marriage is not an end, but a means to an end—self-fulfillment. This arrangement is an improvement.

Other institutions have seen similar metamorphoses. A good example is the change in view towards religious organizations. In the past, people just went to the church of their parents; it was expected. Now people want more. They expect to derive a benefit, or they won't continue attending. The same is true with family life; people want more. Another way to illustrate this difference between institution and relationship is to compare it to the difference between a job and an avocation. A job can be necessary, perfunctory, and uninteresting, while an avocation, which also may be a job, is far more. It holds inherent interest. Many people spend years pursuing an avocation out of love and interest rather than because it is expected of them. Family life has a similar appeal. Whereas in the past people were expected to make sacrifices to preserve the institution, now the individual's self-fulfillment is of paramount importance.

Making self-fulfillment your main purpose in a relationship, however, can have negative consequences. This change in expectations about marriage in itself is not necessarily progress or regression. It's just a change. What is important is that we recognize the change, and that in itself helps minimize difficulties. "Everything will be fine if I can just get married," is naive, myopic thinking. The goal of your partner in marriage is self-fulfillment whether you like it or not. Marriages will not be kept intact at all costs anymore. Individuals live in marriages because they feel more fulfilled by doing so. If they ever come to the realization that this is no longer the case in their marriages, those marriages will probably end. A recognition of this reality will help you to be realistic in your expectations for a marriage. Furthermore, recognizing a partner's motive allows for a greater probability of a successful relationship. By the same token, honest self-assessment of one's motives will help us make better personal decisions, too.

Another positive aspect of this new marriage reality is that individuals today make choices that they want to live in a relationship of marriage rather than feel that it is required or expected of them. It follows then, that the quality of many marriages has improved as a result of this transformation in viewpoint. This is, in fact, what recent surveys show. Individuals want the self-fulfillment associated with marriage and are more apt to work toward preserving the marriage for their own sakes and the sake of the relationship, rather than merely to maintain the marriage as an institution.

Marriage Suggestions

A giant step toward the preservation of a quality marriage and satisfying family life is the recognition of the major deterrent encountered—lack of time. In surveys I've done, respondents admit they do not spend enough time with their families. When asked for suggestions on how family life can be revitalized, again the prime observation is the need for families to spend more time together. Furthermore, sociological studies have discovered one of the prime causes of this lack of time to be the dramatic increase in the number of two-career households. Lifestyle changes, some voluntary and some chosen by circumstances, have contributed to the lack of time. Very often the quality of a marriage or family life will improve simply by realizing what the culprit is—lack of time. More time can be allocated by conscious awareness of our needs.

> **TRANSFORMATION:**
>
> *Marriage is to be viewed as a valuable relationship rather than as an institution.*
>
> "The wife's body does not belong to her alone but also to her husband. In the same way, the husband's body does not belong to him alone but also to his wife." (1 Corinthians 7:4)

Spouses and parents can learn to make adjustments to compensate for time scarcity. A proper valuation of the commodity of time and the choices we make will lead us to ferret out available time for relationship-building.

The Contract

One suggestion that helps a marriage start out on a positive footing and that will help maximize the chances of success in marriage is a "marriage contract." No, I don't mean a prenuptial agreement. I mean, a written agreement between marriage partners, but not one having to do with financial asset allocation. A marriage contract is a private agreement, not necessarily legally binding, that attempts to minimize misunderstandings by the development of a statement as to the couple's joint understanding of their proposed relationship. By putting in writing a statement that both agree upon, misunderstandings are avoided before the marriage becomes legally binding. By discussing in advance some basic issues that must inevitably be encountered in a marriage, the partners can ascertain in which area they are compatible and in which they need to forge a compromise position. If a compromise is not possible in some sensitive and basic areas, it is best that the couple realize this ahead of time. They may decide to rethink their plans.

These are some of the areas couples should thoroughly consider and come to agreement on:

(1) Division of household duties

(2) Preferences for location and type of living quarters

(3) Partner responsibility for child rearing

(4) Sharing of living expenses

(5) Career commitment

(6) Inheritance

(7) Use of surnames

(8) Range of permissible relationships with others

(9) Social obligations

(10) Grounds for divorce

(11) Desire for children and contraception

(12) In-law relations

(13) Leisure activities

(14) Personal values

(15) Provisions for renegotiating the contract

I am not naively asserting that this personal private contract will eliminate all problems. Of course it won't. What it does do, though, is allow a relationship to commence in unity and minimize major problems in the future. The partners have a head start in considering issues they will encounter in the future. They are projecting their relationship into the future and are testing the degree of compatibility. The formation of such an agreement forces the couple to probe into each other's outlook, getting to know each other even better.

Also, remember that such a contract may be revised in time. As the couple continues in personal growth and development, their outlooks may change and may require compromise to preserve compatibility. However, a systematic method of assessing where compromise is needed, such as what I have proposed, is to be preferred over a haphazard and blind departure into the future. So even if you have been married for years, the above checklist is a possible source of topics for continual renewal and reevaluation.

Marriage, A Description

A frank discussion also forces the couple to decide what type of relationship they wish to have. What are they really looking for in marriage? The fact that a couple continues to live together in a marriage does not necessarily identify it as a successful marriage, does it? A well-known study by Cuber and Haroff (1968) found that longtime marriages fall into five categories:

(1) *Conflict-habituated*—there is an acknowledgment by both that incompatibility is pervasive and an atmosphere of tension permeates the relationship.

(2) *Devitalized*—a relationship that started out with a couple deeply in love, but one that has digressed to one where little time is spent together and interests are not shared.

(3) *Passive-congenial*—similar to the devitalized but with the relationship initially formed as an accommodation to both, each having his or her own separate circle of friends.

(4) *Vital*—a close, intimate relationship with partners intensely bound together psychologically. Their sharing and togetherness is a genuine mutuality of feelings.

(5) *Total*—similar to the vital but with more points of meshing, this couple is inextricably linked together and share most activities and interests.

Though these descriptions were written some years ago, they remain appropriate. The question becomes which of these relationships do you want? Success in marriage is not any one of these descriptions; success is more the achieving of the relationship you want. These descriptions give you a catalog of possibilities. The choice is yours. I urge you to make a deliberate choice and then work toward it.

> **TRANSFORMATION:**
>
> *Perfunctory marriage vows need to be supplemented by a well-thought-out written description of what the partners expect in marriage.*

Conflict is inherent in any relationship since opposing dynamics are at work. There is a natural tendency to maintain individuality, but there is also the desire to be part of a group. The two needs don't always mesh. You'll need to exert real effort to achieve the delicate balance. Here is where communication comes into the picture. I hesitate even mentioning the word for fear it will appear trite, but I will say the three qualities that are invariably mentioned as being essential to a good marriage are:

♦ Honesty

♦ Openness with feelings

♦ Mutual consideration for each other as good friends

By working on those three aspects of communication, you can do your part to effect a mutually satisfying relationship. Success in marriage is the attainment of a relationship where each of the partners obtains what he or she wants, where each feels he or she has something of value that could not be attained singly, where each is not being hindered in development but rather where each has his or her growth augmented by the other. That is success, and such success has a wide range of possibilities.

Parenting

One of the basic determinants of the quality of family life is the style and quality of parenting. In this area there is a plethora of manuals overflowing with advice. The sheer volume of this material can be astounding. Unfortunately, parents admit the more they read on parenting, the less confident they are in their ability! Advice is often contradictory and will follow fad themes. I have found, though, that there are only a few basic rules that need to be kept in mind. Parenting does not have to be difficult. Most parents love and want the best for their children. This desire is a motivation toward good parenting. Rather than be swayed by the "experts" whose opinions fluctuate, follow a few basic principles and couple these with your inherent desire to want the best for your offspring.

Few parents consciously recognize that their own personal examples are the most efficient and indelible teachers. Children of all ages observe and tend to mimic the pictures demonstrated by their parents. Many qualities, mannerisms, and habits we demonstrate will be picked up by our children. That fact is elementary, of course. However, how many parents consciously live in such a way that they recognize that what they are doing graphically presents to their children "this is how I want you to act?" Advice on honesty, loyalty, and work ethics we impart by our own examples is almost irresistible and will be readily practiced by children. So as we grow, we grow in our ability to live by the principles we hold to be important, and our children will simultaneously grow. Children come to recognize those same principles to be of paramount importance.

> **TRANSFORMATION:**
>
> *Children learn by example, not by edict.*
>
> "Train a child in the way he should go, and when he is old he will not turn from it." (Proverbs 22:6)

The important word here is consistency. What we teach consistently by example and what we require consistently in practice will become the habits formed by our children. Not only is consistent training readily emulated, but consistency promotes security, a necessary ingredient for stability and growth emotionally, psychologically, and intellectually. To emphasize this point, research indicates that it's not so critical what rules parents insist on as it is for parents to insist on any rules consistently! A stable, learned pattern of behavior, that comes with consistency, will promote security which in turn is a necessary ingredient for meaningful growth.

The three most important elements of a family environment conducive to emotional development of children are:

♦ Love

♦ Discipline

♦ Consistently following predetermined standards

That doesn't appear to be too difficult to provide, does it? Show your children you love them. Prove to them that you really care for them, that you like them as persons, that you appreciate having them around. You are their care givers and not just because you have been delegated this position by society. Rather, you enjoy the responsibility because you like them. You not only care for them, but you care about them! If your child can readily admit to being loved without reservation and that you care enough to take the time to insist on learning and observing certain standards of behavior, a wonderful environment for personal growth has been created!

In school a child is taught, among other things, the three R's. At home he should be taught the three R's that promote security (both physical and psychological) and self-confidence. These three R's are:

(1) Responsibilities

(2) Routines

(3) Requirements

It's easy for a parent to make a resolution that he will first impart to his children what these three R's consist of, but it's quite a different matter to make the effort and have the patience to insist on observation of these standards over a period of time. New Year's resolutions are easily made but not so easily fulfilled. There are times you will be tired, and it will seem a lot easier not to be insistent, but the value of any worthy program is consistency. Consistently insist that your children follow *routines* in the household that provide for organization and a more predictable environment. Consistently insist that all family members follow a set of rules. These *requirements* are rules for dealing with one another and for practical living. They are invaluable elements of socialization that provide children with the basic tools of social interaction necessary to succeed in dealing with others outside the home. Finally, consistently insist that your children recognize and fulfill the responsibilities that each member of the family has. What an invaluable lesson this is, demonstrating that every productive member of society has responsibilities that, when fulfilled, provide a sense of satisfaction and are the bases for feeling useful themselves, important members of society. The three R's can be imparted when children are young and progressively enlarged to include a greater scope of behavior. Again, it's not so important what your definitions of those three R's are as it is to lovingly impart them and insist on their observation.

Parenting Styles

E.E. LeMasters in the work *Parents in Contemporary America: A Sympathetic View* (1977), describes five possible styles of parenting that broadly catalog the possible approaches that can be taken in rearing children. Most parents probably combine several of these categories in their own parenting style, but the descriptions I have listed here very clearly and graphically will help you discern which approaches are most effective. The five parenting styles are:

(1) The Martyr

(2) The Pal

(3) The Police Officer

(4) The Teacher-Counselor

(5) The Athletic Coach

The beauty of these categories is that they instantly provide a description and orientation. Each of us is familiar with the style from our own interaction with these five categories of people. As we discuss these five styles, you'll recognize the advantages and disadvantages of each. Immediately you'll be able to decide which style (or styles) is most appropriate to parenting. I won't need to spend a great deal of time describing them either.

The *martyr* is the parent who would do anything for the child. The parent who waits upon his child, who nags his child, or who buys his child anything and everything is an example. Many negatives associated with this parenting style do not prepare a child for adult life.

The *pal* is the parent who feels she should just be a friend to her child, adopting a limited discipline policy. By allowing the child to set his own rules with minimal guidelines and goals, the parent hopes she can avoid a generation gap. In reality she is setting up her child for future failure. Not only is she neglecting the responsibilities parents in our society are expected to fulfill, but she is unrealistic in expecting that children don't need or deserve the benefit of a parent's greater experience and knowledge. Numerous research papers have associated this style of parenting with delinquency and drug abuse.

The *police officer* is just the opposite. He insists upon discipline much like a drill sergeant would. However, studies have found adolescents are far more likely to be influenced by a desire to identify with the parent's knowledge and values than by the sheer power and authority of the parent. Besides, other studies identify the police officer style with delinquent behavior and drug use. Children (especially adolescents) tend to rebel against the house rules of a strict disciplinarian.

The *teacher-counselor* style of parenting is more amicable. Viewing the child as a person with infinite possibilities to grow, limited only by the parent's ability to provide the proper stimulation and developmental resources, is indeed a positive position. However, this, too, is unrealistic. Parents do have limitations. They are not experts. They cannot be there every minute to provide the appropriate stimulation. It can be harmful to give the child the impression he or she will always be the center of attention to all other people he or she comes in contact with. The guilt *teacher-counselor* parents can feel when they realize they are not all expert psychologists and degreed educators can be discouraging and can dissipate the joy of being a parent.

The fifth style of parenting is the *athletic coach*. This approach stresses the interactive perspective. It also incorporates the positive aspects of the *teacher-counselor* developmental approach but is more realistic. The *coach*, due to age, may not be the epitome of a football quarterback, but he does have the experience and the confidence to demonstrate by example and encourage by word, exhorting his athletes to do their best. Of course, parents are much more than coaches, but we're talking about parenting styles only at this point.

This is the parenting style I suggest parents follow. The *coach* establishes the house rules and then enforces them. Children, as team players, must be taught to accept discipline. The coach wants to bring out the best in his/her players.

The coach also works with the players, listens to them and realizes that all aspects of life will have an effect on the athletes' performance. Once the players are in the game, the coach can't play the game but can encourage and suggest strategy. This is the approach that inherently feels right for me. I often ask myself, "Am I acting as a coach?" The answer readily helps me know what adjustments to make in my behavior as a parent. This question is simple but is a valuable tool for providing direction in my parenting skills. I'm sure you'll find it helpful.

A good coach listens to his players. He develops a sense of belonging in the players— "We're all in this together!" He also roots for and hopes the best for his players. Be a *coach* to your children!

TRANSFORMATION:

Parents can ask themselves, "Am I acting as a coach?"

Guidance Goals

Here's one other piece of advice that I've found most helpful. Again, it's not complicated, but it does produce results far beyond its simplicity. When I've asked parents what they'd like their children to be like when they're on their own, many have had to admit that they'd either never thought about it, or they'd give trite, stereotyped answers. Yet how can anyone build in their children essential qualities without ever having a clear picture of what they're building? Previously, you'll remember, we had a detailed discussion on the necessity and techniques of goal-setting.

This, I have found, is the single most important step in parenting: First ask yourself which important qualities you're attempting to build in your life. Then recognize that those are the qualities you are also attempting to build in your children. Notice I mention *qualities*, not which *material needs*, not which *possessions*, not which *occupational status* but only which *qualities* you wish your children would ultimately possess. If a child-turned-adult has certain qualities, everything else will fall into place. These qualities help them through the difficulties and give them habits, direction, and skills necessary for success in whatever they (not you) decide are their life dreams.

Take the time to think about exactly which qualities you'd like to impart to your children if you could, because you *can*. You need only decide on what they are. Then set these qualities as goals, your own personal goals, to help your children to acquire. There is no reason to specifically tell them what you wish to accomplish. Your own subconscious desire will guide you to guide them. I decided for myself a long time ago what I'd wish for my children, and I've reminded myself regularly. Some of the qualities I chose were the qualities of love and caring, honesty, self-esteem and self-confidence, spirituality, along with an enthusiasm for life, and a desire to be productive members of society. I reasoned that if I could instill these qualities in my own children, I'd have done my part and could be confident that they could adequately take care of themselves as adults.

I urge you as parents to make your list and be very clear as to just what those chosen qualities mean to you. If you put *honesty* on your list, for example, exactly what is honesty to you? You must be specific. Vague ideas cannot be imparted. Then remind yourself of this list often. Let the magic of goal-setting work for you in this arena, too. You'll automatically find yourself emphasizing certain lessons in life and pointing out how this or that quality will help your children in the future. "This sounds too simplistic," you might say. I can guarantee you it's not. Just try it—it works! Just take the first step—make your list, clearly specifying what each item means to you. Then just remind yourself regularly of what you, as their coach, are assisting your children to learn. Be confident that those qualities will be passed on. The few qualities I mentioned above may be similar to the list you'll make for yourself, or you may wish to add a few others. This list is what you'll concentrate on. The other aspects of a competent individual will naturally follow. I can't stress enough what an effective, yet neglected, technique a written statement of goal qualities for your offspring can be. This is part of the legacy you pass on!

Adolescence

I'd like to include one final thought on rearing children, especially as they get into the adolescent years. These can be, by far, the most difficult for both the child and the parent. However, remember what adolescence is—a transition period. Initially, adolescence is a period when children wish for the privileges of adulthood and the limited responsibilities and carefreeness of childhood, simultaneously. Simply understanding this makes adolescence much easier to deal with. Adolescents are searching to discover their true identities, questioning the values of parents, while insisting upon independence from the family. These are healthy and normal steps. Realizing the dynamics of the emotional and intellectual changes taking place in adolescents, parents will not be surprised by the impatient, argumentative, and self-centered nature exhibited. This, too, will pass. Parents can cope with this transition by allowing their adolescents more space and freedom but being available when still needed, all the while accepting that this transition is inevitable and takes time.

The requirements, responsibilities, and routines should definitely not be abandoned just because the children are now adolescents. As a coach, remember you still have more experience in the consequences of actions than your children have. There are some ground rules on which you must tenaciously insist because you are fully aware of the possible dire consequences (drug abuse, unsafe sex), while allowing more discretion in areas that are not as critical, such as appearance. Communicate these basic ground rules and also communicate your love and real interest in their welfare. I promise you it will work!

Divorce

What a paradox to observe that marriage has probably never been more meaningful than it is today (it's not just a ritual, it's a relationship), yet divorce is more prevalent than ever. Spouses often are no longer willing to tolerate a relationship in which they are not deeply involved and from which they do not readily feel the benefits that should accrue. This can be considered a positive development. Also, there are many more avenues available to seek help for a wavering marriage. Resources such as counseling, group sessions, and classes are now available. That, too, is a positive development in society.

However, there are negatives to divorce. I'm afraid that frequently divorce is considered as an option without weighing the negative consequences. Divorce is a major (if not *the* major) stressor in a world already overflowing with stress that has a deleterious effect on our minds, emotions, and bodies. Is divorce the only alternative? In some cases, it may be, but the decision must be made cautiously.

Divorce does affect children, especially young children. Don't allow sage articles to sugarcoat the consequences. Realize that studies invariably show negative consequences among many children. Statistics show that roughly one-third of children will cope successfully with the experience; another 30 percent will cope unevenly with the experience (meaning that sometimes they'll do well with periods of difficulty), and 39 percent remain moderately to severely depressed even five years after the divorce (Wallerstein and Kelly, 1980). The more recent statistics are more explicit and clear on outcomes—children are hurt by divorce. It's true that statistics are open to interpretation as to why children are hurt, and my purpose is not to debate these but only to point out that parents considering a divorce must make the decision being fully aware that there will probably be negative consequences for their children. Are you prepared to accept this rather than to blindly deny that there could be problems?

> **TRANSFORMATION:**
>
> *Successful family living requires a delicate balance between group needs (loyalty) and individual needs (individualism).*
>
> "For the Lord loves the just and will not forsake his loyal ones." (Psalms 37:28)

Divorce is such a complex issue that it cannot be adequately dealt with here. There are myriad books that will help you learn from the experiences of others and how they learned to cope. If you are dealing with this issue, Chapter 12 on "Balance" can help you to get through any such difficult period.

Please note that the popular views of society cannot be used as gauges in making serious decisions that will have awesome effects on you and your children. In the past, society put the emphasis on preserving the group (family) while considering the individual's interest of secondary importance. The pendulum has swung in the opposite direction now with individual welfare paramount regardless of the consequences. Let's remember that there will always be a need in society for a delicate balance between such dynamic and opposing concepts as group needs versus individual needs and individual rights versus individual responsibility.

You must develop this delicate balance as it applies to you. Society will periodically put the emphasis on one side or the other of the dynamic equation, but you, as an individual, must live with the choices you make.

Activity

Take time now to review the decisions this chapter has suggested you make. Specifically set objectives for yourself using the lists provided in this chapter.

♦ What type of marriage do you wish to have?

♦ What elements do you wish to incorporate in your marriage contract?

♦ What parenting styles will you choose to emulate?

♦ What life qualities do you hope to impart as a legacy?

Conclusion

I hope that you will encounter each event in family life, whether it be marriage, the decision to be a parent, or the possibility of divorce with a full grasp of the possibilities available. Make these decisions with deliberation rather than allowing the choices to be made for you. Meaningful family life is both a joy and a necessity for personal growth. Open yourself to the possibilities but recognize the inherent responsibilities. You will then experience the sense of belonging and feel part of the legacy that family life perpetuates.

"A man travels the world over in search of what he needs and returns home to find it." (George Moore)

"But as for me and my household, we will serve the Lord" (Joshua 24:15)

CHAPTER 7

Abundant Affluence (Fortune)

I remember being ten years old and marveling that some of my schoolmates could have soda pop when they came home from school or whenever they wished. In my house, soda pop was a luxury that I'd seen maybe once in those ten years. I was raised in a blue-collar family, but, like many who have had similar circumstances have found, it turned out to be a blessing. I learned the value of financial assets, and I was determined that I was not going to stay poor. I was going to have soda pop whenever I wished, and I was going to have a new baseball mitt, not the hand-me-down model I had. You know, the kind that looked like an oversized glove with five fingers and no lacing. To me that's what being successful meant, having those few luxuries. I wasn't asking for much. It was years later that I understood it took little more effort to be affluent rather than to just get by. I was introduced to some of the basic principles of wealth-building by a friend after I was married and had my own family. Over time, I refined a few simple rules for affluence I've lived by ever since.

By the end of this chapter you can be, in fact, you *should* be wealthy! This is not impossible. This is not hype. If you read carefully, understand the principles well, and really believe them, you will be wealthy from that moment on! I know you may not believe this now, but be patient.

Many self-improvement texts treat financial matters in conjunction with career. I, however, feel that though they are related, they have very different focuses. Career counseling has to do with earning money and enjoying yourself while you go about doing so. Affluence and wealth are how you use your money and more importantly, how you view your money. This is the key to acquiring abundance—your view of money and wealth. By understanding a few important concepts, you'll gain career success and all your material desires as a natural consequence of those beliefs and actions.

Among Christians in general, wealth has had a rather negative connotation. To some, Christianity means one must almost take a vow of poverty. This interpretation cannot be further from the truth. The Bible admonishes that putting trust in wealth is foolish as is illustrated by the story of the man who spent his life amassing riches only to be told he would die before he could fully enjoy what he had. (Luke 12:17-21) One of the foundation premises of this book is the importance for balance in all things. This is the lesson behind all the cautions given in Scripture about being overly concerned with money. Jesus stated it clearly at the end of his story of the ill-fated rich man. "That is how it is with the man who amasses wealth for himself and remains a pauper in the sight of God." (Luke 12:21) However, a Christian believes as St. Paul says in Romans 18:17, "We are God's heirs and Christ's fellow-heirs." Christians believe and act as heirs to the inestimable fortune of their Heavenly Father. As heirs, they have access to that fortune. As Jesus himself promised, "If you ask anything in my name, I will do it." (John 14:14) If you are a Christian you may not have the proper outlook unless you fully believe you are privileged and wealthy at this moment! Being wealthy is just a matter of the proper attitude. As a Christian you are joint-heirs with Christ, heirs of a universe of treasures. Having access to such astonishing wealth, how could you possibly go around considering yourself poor? For those of you who don't have this Christian perspective yet, or for those not Christian, I'm going to set out clearly the principles for availing yourself of the fortune that can rightly belong to you.

A Revelation of Riches

To begin, let's be clear about what wealth is. Wealth is that which is valuable to you. True wealth is both possessing and enjoying what is of great worth to you. True affluence means having the ability to acquire whatever you want; whatever you dream of or desire fervently becomes yours if you are truly wealthy. You are affluent if you possess or can have at any time the things of value that will bring you happiness. So, wealth is the *ability* to have what you truly desire. This is a critical point that is seldom understood.

Let's consider one person who has amassed a net worth of several million dollars but denies himself the things that would help him find happiness. Then observe another person who doesn't have as great a monetary accumulation but always has what she wishes. If she has a desire for a new car, she buys one. If she wishes for a vacation in Hawaii, she takes it. She knows that whatever she wants she invariably receives it. Which individual is truly wealthy here? What is the critical difference? The difference is attitude toward ability. If you don't have the ability to acquire what you want, you can't be wealthy regardless of the amount of money you may have in a bank account. If your constitution or your mental outlook won't allow you to use this money for the things you want, you are not affluent. What's worse, you're actually a pauper! If you have a mental viewpoint that causes you to deny yourself or continually put off acquiring what you want, you don't have wealth.

Wealth, then, is the ability to have what you value and to enjoy it. You may have whatever you desire, but if your outlook does not allow you to enjoy it, you are not wealthy. Rather than saying, "Power is wealth," it is, "Wealth is power," power simply being the ability to get things done as you wish.

Balance is the critical concept in this definition of wealth. Wealth is the ability to acquire and to enjoy. Contentment is tantamount to wealth. To feel settled about what you desire and possess is indeed an enviable state. Wealth is a mental outlook more than anything else. To recognize that you already have the resources necessary to possess whatever you wish and to be able to enjoy those possessions free from worry and guilt but with the satisfaction that you deserve them—this is true wealth.

Let's look at the two aspects of the mental outlook of the wealthy, separately. With regard to ability to acquire possessions, let me ask this: Is there any difference in an actual material possession, like a car, if purchased with cash from your bank account, or if the money were given to you as a present, or if you pay for the car in installments from your weekly paycheck? The car is exactly the same no matter how you acquire it, isn't it? You have it; it's yours. You can have the enjoyment of driving it regardless of the source of the funds used to purchase it. If you are convinced that whenever you really desired a possession (like a specific car or boat) the funds would always be there; this is having true riches. Such confidence is actually a mental and emotional outlook. *The confidence that the funds are always available and that we have the ability to acquire is the first aspect of wealth.* It is a state of mind. In a moment we will discuss how we go about acquiring this state of mind of confidence in our ability to acquire what we desire. At this point, I hope you can begin to see that your first step to becoming wealthy is to develop the proper wealth consciousness.

The second point is that even if we had a million dollars in the bank and bought a new car but somehow felt we didn't deserve it, we couldn't really enjoy it to the full. If we felt guilty that this was too extravagant or the funds should not have been used for our own pleasure, again, the enjoyment that should go with the possession would be lost. This, too, is a state of mind, isn't it?

> **TRANSFORMATION:**
> *Wealth is a state of mind, the confidence that we will always have the funds for what we need or want.*
>
> "You may ask me for anything in my name, and I will do it." (John 14:14)

Let's say one of your work associates carries with him a "rain cloud" pessimism wherever he goes. You know the type, always able to conjure up the most negative, unlikely scenario for any event. You also work with someone who is always able to muster up a cheerful, "I feel good about what's going to happen today." Who do you think will succeed in his position? Your prediction is not based on ability, is it? The attitude exhibited will usually be the determinant. I'm saying that affluence works the same way. *An expectant attitude toward wealth will attract such riches to your life!*

Your Own Prosperity

You can acquire a wealth state of mind and all the possessions that are commensurate with it. First of all, we see evidence of the prosperity in nature all around us. The beauty of natural settings and the bounty of mankind's creations are before us everywhere. These are all evidence of the power of the universe or the power of God. Each of us is part of this universe or a product of God's mind. Just knowing we are a part of the same universal family and the same creation of God should immediately boost our self-esteem. As a member of the family, you are entitled to the inheritance. By virtue of your being you, you are worthy to enjoy the abundance of the universe. You have a right to enjoy and take pleasure in the riches that exist as much as anyone else. You need only fervently want these possessions and follow the steps that are necessary to take possession of them, and they are yours.

I remember when my children were young, they wanted every new toy they saw at the store. I frequently bought them what they wanted but discovered that the pleasure diminished the more they had. They wanted everything at once, all at that very moment, even though they could only play with so many toys at one time. Collecting toys that they didn't really enjoy didn't make sense and didn't bring contentment. I learned it was best to tell them, "You may have whatever you want as long as you really want it." I meant it, too. As long as I was sure they truly desired a toy, I made sure they got it sooner or later. One of the ways I could tell if they really wanted a toy was, if after some time passed, they still felt they just had to have it. I learned to tell them, "If you still want it next week (or next month), you may have it."

It was interesting to see how many momentary desires fell by the wayside. I also noticed that the toys they were persistent in asking for usually turned out to be the ones they played with the most. I learned from bringing my children up what wealth really is. *Wealth means knowing you can have whatever you want without having to worry about how you will pay for it,* even as my children did not have to worry about how they would pay for whatever they wanted. They only had to decide that they really wanted something. Their desires were fulfilled, but patience was required. The same is true for all of us! Patience is required. Whatever you desire you can have as long as you truly want it. One way you know you really want something is if you're willing to patiently take the steps necessary to get those things. If not, that thing must not have been that important to you after all.

I've seen this happen often. Ted had a dream of owning a BMW automobile. His had to be white with black leather interior in a particular model. Based on his salary at the time, it was really beyond his means. That didn't stop him from dreaming. He persisted. In fact his friends would tease him about his *obsession*, they'd call it. Ted didn't know how it would happen; he just knew it would happen. In a matter of eight months though, a departmental supervisor position became available. Ted applied and won the promotion. One of the first things he did after getting new business cars was to order his BMW. He had to order it specifically since the dealership didn't have the model in the exact detail Ted had envisioned, and he wouldn't settle for any deviation. Ted's friends no longer tease him; they admire his tenacity.

Marlene's dream took a little longer to materialize. I remember shortly after we got married, my wife began a scrapbook of her dream house. She'd get magazines like *Better Homes and Gardens* and cut out pictures of the furniture, the window treatments, the house designs, landscaping ideas, anything that caught her attention. This was back when I was a janitor. I don't think Marlene ever thought she would live in such a house. At the time it was just a hobby, a diversion. But she persisted, cutting out pictures and articles. From time to time, she'd show me a picture that would catch her attention. How the money for these projects would come, I can attest, never bothered her. She never prodded me to increased business success. But with each successive move we made, she'd incorporate more of her ideas. Only years later did I realize that she saw her vision become a reality. I commented, "You know, the way you have this house decorated, it would easily be a candidate for *Better Homes and Gardens.*" Over the years, though styles and treatments have changed, her dream house looks remarkably similar to her initial dreams. Though she has experimented with various styles, she's always come back to the traditional look that originally began her dreaming. I can attest that Marlene never obsessed over how to get the money. She just had fun with her hobby, but that hobby has become a reality.

I've observed time and again that once you know what you truly want, you are automatically guided to learn what you should be doing to attain it. As you advance steadfastly in the direction you realize you must go, the desired possessions become more apparent and more certain of attainment. This is the process I described in detail in the chapter on goal orientation. This is a universal mechanism that comes into operation once a single-minded goal is proposed and believed worthy of your effort. I have taught my children what I have learned, some of which I've learned indirectly from them—I can have whatever I want if I'm willing to do what is required to have it and as long as I don't squander it. You can have this wealth-consciousness, too. If within you is a fervent desire for something, you'll gladly take the steps necessary to get it. Often people act like young children, though, flitting from one "toy" to the next, not really enjoying anything to the full, and never pausing long enough to ask, "Is this what I want?"

To be truly rich, first be certain through soul searching and meditation what you fervently want, recognizing that so many of the riches we want are easily attainable. I realized that knowledge and understanding of life were among the most valuable things to me. Once I realized that, I knew what steps I'd patiently have to take. I was confident that I would attain this affluence as long as I persevered. I also realized I could have any number of riches I wanted if I followed a similar regimen.

This is true for anyone. However, as adults, we realize what young children still have not learned. We can play with only so many "toys" at one time. There comes a point where we waste and squander the resources of the earth and universe when we don't enjoy the things we have. Wealth is having the *confidence* that we can have whatever we want and having the *wisdom* to take the time to enjoy what we have. It's best that we decide what things we truly want before cluttering our lives with things about which we don't really care. If material riches are truly our desire, we'll be led to the steps we need to take, whether those steps be the search for a higher-paying job or the pursuit of a specialized career skill. Be patient and follow the steps. Then, once you have acquired the material desires, enjoy them, knowing you paid the necessary price to attain them—therefore you deserve them.

Mental Wealth

One aspect of a wealth mindset is the elimination of confusion. With so many possibilities in life, with so much abundance and variety around us, where do we start? Philosophers through the ages have begged us to learn what they have observed—the true course to tapping the abundance of nature and life is to simplify our lives by eliminating the confusion that comes from having too many choices. I stressed this in the Chapter 3 on goal-setting.

Moreover, a critical aspect of the proper mindset is the confidence that you deserve part of the riches the universe displays. There is more than enough for all to have what they want. We all deserve this affluence. It's never a question of whether or not we can afford it. We are members of the universal family, and as family members, we hold claim to the family inheritance! The recurring theme throughout self-development literature of the past thirty years is the need to rethink our life situation and truly believe we are as worthy of wealth as anyone. Once we realize we are not chosen for poverty, and there is no logical reason we should not share in life's prosperity, we need only assume the things we desire will naturally come to us in time, though patience may be needed.

Even if you had the cash to pay for a Rolls Royce, for example, it could take months before you took possession of it since it might have to be built to your specifications and shipped. That takes time. In such a case, you would be willing to be patient because you knew what you wanted, you ordered it, and you're merely waiting for it to be built. Really, this scenario is true with whatever you genuinely want. If you have "ordered" it in your mind, whatever it is, you need only be patient to see its materialization.

TRANSFORMATION:

Mental wealth is the recognition that we are just as deserving of riches as anyone else in the world.

"Look at the birds of the air; they do not sow or reap or store away in barns, and yet your heavenly Father feeds them. Are you not much more valuable than they?" (Matthew 6:26)

"Simply" Abundant

Now that you understand the concept of wealth, let's share some practical suggestions for the accumulation of the monetary reserves necessary to finance the purchases and possessions you desire. One caution: more is never enough! If you allow yourself to get into the mindset that "if only I can just get this, I'll be satisfied..." you begin programming yourself to have fulfillment continually elude you. "Fulfillment will come with the next acquisition" is a mindset which works at cross-purposes with the desire for contentment. I suggest you first take stock of what you *do* have, decide which of your possessions you truly enjoy. Which of those things are genuinely appreciated? Recognize that you already have at least some things, perhaps many, that provide a measure of satisfaction in your life. Now, build on those feelings of fulfillment. Making a physical summary of your possessions forces you to be appreciative and to get off the ever-moving merry-go-round of "more" mentality. Which things right now

bring you the greatest pleasure? Are they necessarily material possessions? You already have the necessities for this happiness within you. Happiness will not come from more possessions if you are
not content within yourself, first knowing that you have the faculties within you that will bring you whatever you want.

Wealth-consciousness does not begin on the material level.
Wealth is far more than material things. Yes, wealth can include
abundant physical possessions if desired, but that is only the tip
of the iceberg. That is what can be seen. Numerous belongings
may be a manifestation of wealth, but wealth is much more. The
word wealth comes from the root word "weal" which means well-
being. Well-being, that's what we're really striving for when we
try to achieve wealth. Well-being relates to a mental, emotional,
spiritual, and physical state of contentment and satisfaction. We
can have the latter (well-being) without the former (material manifestation). Often, though, with the well-being comes the accumulation of the material things that are wished. This state of mind
I'm suggesting, the state of physical well-being, is first and fore-
most related to your thinking.

Next, if you think in terms of prosperity in your life, prosperity will be drawn to you. Be conscious of the continual intrusion
of the contagious negativity of society. Daily, people around you
will speak in terms of limitations: "I can't do this." "I don't have
enough funds for that." "I'm just barely making it." This is a *lack*
mentality. If you find you're mired in this rut, it can be difficult to
extricate yourself. Remember that the goal-striving mechanism
will attract to you that which you think about and plan. If you
inadvertently accept lack thinking, your thought processes will go
that way: "I don't have enough, I can't afford it." In thinking that
way, you've already made a choice, perhaps an unconscious one,
that you don't or won't ever have the resources. The frightening
thing may be that you don't feel you deserve more.

It's just as easy (and much more enjoyable!) to flip the switch
and begin thinking in a prosperity mode. "I *can* have whatever I
want. I deserve what I've chosen as a goal in my life. There is
such abundance in nature around me, why should I be denied the

things I really desire? They can belong to me if I wish." It's that simple. Just consciously flip the switch and see how life around you automatically conforms to your expectations. You'll begin to notice instances where life now aligns to help rather than hinder you. This is prosperity mentality. "I am prosperous," you begin to say. "There is an infinite amount of prosperity in the world around me, and I can have my share."

> **TRANSFORMATION:**
>
> *Replace **lack** mentality with **prosperity** mentality.*
>
> "If you, then, though you are evil, know how to give good gifts to your children, how much more will your Father in heaven give good gifts to those who ask him!?" (Matthew 7:11)

Material Suggestions

The problem with many texts on wealth accumulation is that they deal only with accumulation on a material level while the far more powerful mental and spiritual levels are neglected. Emphasize the mental-positive prosperity mindset. Dwell only sparingly on the gross material plane. So far I have dealt only with this superior level. Dealing from this level will immediately cause changes in your life. But here are a few suggestions from a material level to be certain you are familiar with techniques for material wealth accumulation once you have begun to think in a prosperity mode. But don't analyze wealth only from this lower plane.

Funds Accumulation

Let's tackle the idea of accumulating a fund of money. Remember that the purpose of a fund is not to just collect large piles of currency for yourself; it's to gain the accouterments that go along with money. A monetary fund represents security, options, hope, peace of mind, confidence, and charity. So when setting a goal of X amount of dollars you'd like to accumulate, think in terms of the above concepts. Those ideas will excite and motivate you. Then use the technique discussed in the chapter on goal-setting to accomplish your desires.

We've probably all heard about the idea of saving 10 percent of whatever we earn as a good method of accumulation. However, this just doesn't work if you're saving without a goal for that money. It's better to set goals for saving money. Saving for a down payment on a car, a home mortgage down payment, or the security of a carefree retirement are much more motivating ideas.

It's best to save long-term by placing your funds in a vehicle that will accumulate tax-free rather than have valuable interest income siphoned off by income tax. Therefore, make use of pension accounts through your employer. 401K plans where your employer will match your savings are even better, but at least make use of an IRA. Though those in higher income levels cannot deduct all they would like to contribute to their Individual Retirement Account (IRA), at least by setting aside the maximum investment each year in such an account, the funds accumulate at a much faster rate since their build-up is protected from current taxes.

Furthermore, the power of compound interest can never be minimized. Even at a low interest rate of 5 percent, any person investing regularly $600 per month will build a sizable nest egg of $100,000 in ten years. The magic of regular, timely savings and the compounding of interest will result in financial growth and security.

Debts

Probably the best starting point for financial security is to take stock of and reduce debts that have been creeping upward. Almost everyone has too much debt; it's almost become a way of life. However, the good news is that just about everyone can get out from under the oppression of debts in approximately fourteen months. The money now used to make installment payments on credit card debts and other charge accounts can then be deferred toward savings once the debt is systematically eliminated. The process to use is quite simple.

First, make a list of what you owe. Maybe you've been avoiding it. But to conquer any problem the first step is to face it realistically. The typical person will usually have large credit card balances charging 20 percent or more in finance charges. By allowing this to continue, you allow the magic of compound interest to work against you. These self-perpetuating debts insidiously deny you from building your personal net worth. Once your debts are listed, begin systematically to pay off each credit card or company charge, one at a time. Pay off first the ones with the lowest balances. Then use that monthly payment that you had been regularly paying and apply it to the next credit card balance.

For example, you may have seven or eight open accounts, each requiring a minimum payment monthly of anywhere from $25 to $100 or more. Start with the one where you have the lowest balance (and probably the lowest monthly payment), and decide to make only your minimum payments the first month on all your credit account balances, but pay an extra amount on that one lowest balance, let's say $100. Once that account is paid off, you are then in a position to pay $100, plus whatever that minimum installment had been (let's say $25) toward the next lowest account balance. $125, plus that account's regular minimum payment, will pay it off early. Once paid, you can then afford to pay $125, plus the next account's minimum balance ($50, for example), or $175 toward the third credit card balance. This systematic process works, and since it will take only a little over one year, or at the most two, you will stick with it.

To decide what that first extra amount must be, remember these two figures. It takes two years to pay off each $1,000 owed on a 20 percent finance charge account if $50 per month is paid. It takes one year to pay off that $1,000 on a similar account if you pay $90 per month toward it. So if you owe $5,000, and you want to pay it off in two years, it will require that you pay five times $50, or $250, a month. Use that $250 as the starting point to gauge what must be paid toward all open accounts, along with all minimum balances, to retire bill debt in two years. When using this procedure, choose only one credit card to charge new purchases and pay them off monthly. By paying back an amount greater than your aggregate monthly debt note each month and systematically paying off one account at a time, debt can be eliminated. Once accomplished, this money can then be used to start a savings plan.

Getting Your Time's Worth

One technique that will help you get off the "more" mentality merry-go-round, is to think in terms of money as a measure of time. You have invested a period of time in order to acquire the money needed to finance a purchase. Have you gotten your "time's worth?" In other words, when you buy a new leather coat, how many hours did you have to work or will you have to work for that article of clothing? Is having that possession worth the time you gave for the purchase? For example, let's say you take home $30,000 yearly in income. That $30,000 is an indication that your work life is worth $30,000 divided by fifty-two weeks, divided by forty hours per week; thus each hour of work is measured by $15 of income. Therefore, what you buy can be translated into hours. A $60 shirt cost you four hours of work. Now ask yourself, "Was it worth it?" When it comes time to make a purchase, ask yourself if it's worth X number of hours of your work life. This thinking helps us raise ourselves above the pure material level; it forces us to examine what is really impor-

> **TRANSFORMATION:**
>
> *Money is a measure of the time required to be given in exchange for material possessions.*

tant to us; it helps us to avoid wasting and squandering the resources around us. This thinking also helps us to free up funds for what's truly important to us. Is it worth one day of work life to pay $15 x 8 = $120 for a new knickknack? If so, go ahead; it's worth it. If not, forgo the purchase with a feeling of satisfaction that you just freed up funds for something more important or something for which you would gladly exchange one day of life work.

I caution you to use the technique just discussed only for material possessions. Any purchases that can be viewed as an investment in your future are almost always worth the price. Any purchase, for instance, that will enhance your education, health, or self-esteem is to be viewed as an investment that should almost always be followed through, even if it means borrowing to do so. These types of investments will pay dividends many times over. If a $400 business suit will enhance your self-esteem, by all means get it immediately. This investment in yourself will be paid back shortly by the increased career success that is forthcoming.

> ### TRANSFORMATION:
> *Any purchase or savings that can be considered an investment in yourself is a priority.*
>
> "Remember this: Whoever sows sparingly will also reap sparingly, and whoever sows generously will reap generously."
> (2 Corinthians 9:6)

The same is true of education. Recently I read that a college graduate earns on an average of $10,000 a year more than someone with only a high school diploma. In an average working life of forty years, with raises, that means an extra $1 million or more to the college graduate, directly attributable to his or her education investment. Even in purely material terms, the cost of a college education is repaid many times over. The cost of vocational training is also a good investment. Money is no object when you invest in yourself. Here are the questions to ask regarding a purchase:

- ♦ Is it worth the hours of life I've given in exchange for it?
- ♦ Is it an investment in myself?
- ♦ Will it enhance my education, health, or self-esteem?

These questions will help you decide whether you should go ahead with a purchase.

Savings

The important point about saving is having the proper view. Savings is not to be viewed as a limitation on spending. Savings is a means to reach important objectives. Savings is buying a new home; savings is a secure retirement; savings is the education of your children and affording a new luxury car. So if you haven't already, change your mindset of savings to make it goal-oriented. Each fund (you should have a number of savings funds accumulating at one time) should represent a clear objective, along with a monetary value set; therefore it is ambitious.

Follow this simple process. Pick a long- or short-term goal, set a realistic monetary value on that goal, and decide how to build up the fund. Some goals, such as a comfortable retirement, may be difficult on which to set a financial value without professional advice. This is when you'll want to call on a financial planner or investment advisor to help you quantify your goal. Always put a specific value on a goal, remembering the principles discussed in Chapter 3 on goal-setting.

I don't intend to get into investment strategies, but suffice it to say, you as a goal-minded saver, have a choice. Either you develop the financial acumen to set a financial strategy for fund-accumulation, or you consult a financial planner for expertise in this area. The principles of (1) elimination or limitation of current taxes, and (2) diversification of savings portfolios need to be clearly addressed regardless of the avenues taken to accumulate savings.

Activity

♦ Decide whether you accept the idea that you are as worthy as anyone else to attain affluence.

♦ Decide realistically what wealth means to you, recognizing that the satisfaction level will be different for different people.

➡ What do you need to be satisfied?

♦ Decide what kind of changes will be necessary to meet your personal picture of what wealth is.

➡ Will changes need to be made merely at the accounting level?

➡ Will regular promotions in your field accommodate your desires for material possessions?

➡ Will a major shift in career direction such as awakening the entrepreneurial spirit within you be the only conceivable course capable of satisfying your personal needs?

♦ Decide whether you are willing to sacrifice the necessary time and energy to attain the level of financial security that will satisfy you.

Refer to Chapter 3 on goal-setting for suggestions to implement your resolve.

What I Learned

In this section I've stressed the changes in mindset necessary to be functioning optimally in the finance arena of your life. At times, it's just a minor shift that's necessary. I had such an experience. One of the concepts I stressed is the elimination of the negative "I can't afford it" mindset. I realized that I had inherited this demoralizing belief. My parents had lived through the Depression. The only way they survived was by economizing, being extremely frugal, and denying themselves present pleasures. I inherited this mindset, limiting the joy that I could have in life. I found it necessary to reconcile the positives of frugality that had been ingrained in me since childhood with the negative aspects of stinginess. Through mental searching I realized that wealth consciousness and frugality were not mutually exclusive for me. Yes, I could afford whatever I wished. I didn't need to scrimp. I then reconstructed "frugality" to mean the need to watch that I did not waste resources. In this age of ecology-mindedness, this shift in thinking has been easy.

By meditating on this, I have been able to reconcile a newfound wealth mentality with an inherited respect for frugality—with just a minor shift in thinking. I can and do have a new car whenever I wish, but I temper this desire with the positive principle of eliminating the waste of natural resources. Nature has inexhaustible recyclable resources as long as they are not squandered. I have learned never to be cheap or spartan, but I also realize that since I can have whatever I want whenever I want, there is no need to go on a continuous spending spree. I purchase a new luxury automobile regularly since I don't want to waste time on frequent repairs, but I don't need one each year. The time spent shopping for new cars can be used much more productively elsewhere. Besides, since I know I could have a new one whenever I wish, I am perfectly content keeping one model until it begins to show the signs of wear. I then recycle it, offering it to someone who enjoys working on cars or who would rather not pay for a new car. A negative mindset was not for me; it's not for you either!

Review

The riches of life:
♦ Nature has no limitations to the abundance it will share with me.
♦ I deserve to liberally use the storehouses of nature.
♦ I can afford whatever I wish.
♦ There is no such thing as "I can't afford it."
♦ I use and enjoy but never squander the wealth of nature.
♦ I regularly invest financially in myself.

*"Ask and it will be given to you;
seek and you will find..." (Matthew 7:7)*

"Blessings and prosperity will be yours." (Psalm 128:2)

CHAPTER 8

Nurturing Networks (Friends)

Not until I lost almost all my friends did I comprehend what a privilege it is to call someone a friend and to count on friends for help in adversity. I just assumed friends were automatic, but, as you know, that isn't so. When I made a decision that I was going to further my education and not follow the lead of my factory worker friends, I wasn't prepared for the consequences. I had made a decision to go to college after a number of years away from school, years when I survived on manual labor and had assumed the beliefs and expectations of my friends. However, when I tried to break the mold, I wasn't prepared for the rejection I received. I imagine my "friends" thought I was abandoning them. Maybe I thought I was too good for them. How dare I repudiate the simplistic mentality that they and I had felt comfortable with! I didn't see it coming, perhaps because I was so wrapped up in my new pursuits, but the next thing I knew, I hadn't many friends left. I had to start over making a new set of friends. I no longer fit in with my former crowd, and they made that clear by their half-hearted greetings when they saw me on the street and the few invitations I received to stop over for an evening. One year I had to go to a restaurant just to have people around me to watch the Superbowl (my wife is not a sports fan). That was a low point for me. I vowed I'd never take friends for granted again. I hope, for most of you, this will never have to happen, but you can learn from what I did to find and cultivate new friendships.

Friendship...what a beautiful thing! There are few experiences more gratifying than having close friends who are really interested in your welfare. A strong friendship endures difficulties and misunderstandings and looks beyond immediate benefits. There are things you can do to nurture enduring, trusting, and confidential friendships. Loyalty, for example, allows the bonds of mutual admiration to grow first from the seeds of respect into the strong ties of mutual acceptance and mutual growth. In this chapter we'll explore some of the habits you can practice to find and grow friendships.

King David said of his friend, Jonathan, "Jonathan, my brother, dear and delightful you were to me. Your love for me was wonderful, surpassing the love of women." (2 Samuel 1:25, New English Bible) This epitome of a friendship that was demonstrated by David and Jonathan provides a worthy picture for us. Friends require mutual admiration and a desire to maintain a relationship. Friendships like theirs inherently include: kindness, love, caring, and loyalty. Jonathan admired David's abilities and military prowess but evidently saw beyond his accomplishments and recognized his inner strength and devotion to the spiritual aspects of life. Jonathan was heir to the throne of his father, Saul, and could have viewed David as his chief rival but did not. When his father, Saul, attempted to kill David to eliminate a would-be usurper of the throne, Jonathan loyally stood by David, even though doing so put his own life in danger. Unfortunately, as loyalty has waned as a stellar quality, so has the quality of many friendships.

> *"The crown of these*
> *Is made of love and friendship, and sits high*
> *Upon the forehead of humanity." (John Keats)*

Research studies are continually showing that close relationships even promote better health, longer life, and more successful personal goal-attainment. A study at Duke University of some 1,300 people having suffered heart attacks found that the patients who did not have a close relationship with at least one other person (be it a spouse or close confidant) had a death rate three times as high as those who had such a friendship. Other studies have shown that happily married individuals report fewer health difficulties and noticeably fewer aches and pains and are less likely to have bouts with depression. Finally, research reported by one of the early self-help authors, Napoleon Hill, reported that the highly successful business magnates of his time almost invariably attributed an appreciable amount of their success to their having a loyal, encouraging spouse who helped them through temporary set-backs. Such positive relationships, whether it be between spouses or simply good friends, is priceless.

Though we inherently admire the loyalty that is the cement of these relationships, the practice of loyalty doesn't appear to be diligently cultivated today. This may be due to the "me first" philosophy of the late 1970s and early 1980s or the apparent acceptance that selfishness is in one's best interest. However, there is something to be said for the quality of friendships that has been prized throughout the annals of literature as being a cornerstone of social progress—and one of the very reasons for it. The emphasis today on personal happiness at all costs, regardless of the effects on others, is an affront to the striving and progress of humanity nurtured by loyalty. From a long-term view, surely the evidence would support the premise that loyalty not only is in the best interest of society but of the individual as well. Certainly the medical and social research of our time supports this premise. Relationships that are built upon loyalty take effort and do not endure automatically. Difficulties must be endured. At times, self-interest must be set aside in the interest of fostering relationships. The result is worthy of the effort, though. To have someone care meticulously for your welfare when you're going though difficulties is an inexplicable joy. And to care for others you love brings a special bliss.

The three basic questions about friendships that we'll want to explore are, "Where do you find them? How do you initiate and build them? How do you keep them?"

Where?

If you are seeking a satisfying relationship, whether it be with someone of the opposite sex or simply finding a personal confidant, one basic principle has been borne out by statistical research and common sense. People relate to those who are similar to them. This means that people gravitate to others with a similar background, similar interests, or similar outlook on life. To find a relationship you need only go to places where others of similar interest or disposition congregate. This means if your interests are in sports, you will find others with much in common at athletic clubs and sporting events. If your interest is in academic growth, you will find others of similar interests at an adult education class at a community college or university. To attain lasting relationships, you must first be honest with yourself and then be honest with your would-be friends. How foolish to look for friends at the corner bar if you have nothing in common with such people! Similarly, to join a civic group to meet people, though you have no interest in such matters, is equally foolish. You will find short-term friendships or cordial acquaintances at such places, but these are not enduring friendships.

A good place to find individuals with whom you would feel privileged to associate might be at a community service group. Special interest clubs are also a good place to start. Seeking out a formal organization where you can feel part of a group and experience camaraderie allows you to meet with others in a structured environment. There the burden is not on you alone to initiate a friendship. The formal organization structure takes care of that for you. So even if you are shy, you need not feel it's solely up to you to forge a friendship. It will happen as a matter of course. The important thing is to find a group related to your interests. This means being realistic with yourself first. Fortunately, there are groups for any number of diverse interests: environmental groups, volunteer service groups, literary clubs, sports car enthusiasts, church groups; you need only choose something in which you are truly interested, and you will immediately have a legitimate tie to others who attend.

Building

The next step in building a relationship is to resolve to do what is necessary to change your behavior, if need be, to accommodate friends. One important skill is the ability to listen to others. It may be necessary at first to force yourself to listen to someone, listening till they are through speaking before stepping in to speak yourself, or listening before making a hasty decision that this person has nothing of interest for you. Everyone has an interesting story, has something to say worthy of your attention. When you show others that you recognize in them something of worth, they respond to you. When you show your appreciation for them, they, in turn, inevitably show appreciation to you. This is a rule of life: "You receive back what you give, and in the measure you have given." (Luke 6:38)

The important point, though, is not to focus on the benefits you are giving or receiving. Volunteer or work with a group because you truly enjoy it. Concentrate on feeling part of a team. Bask in the accomplishment of being part of a close camaraderie rather than on the specific benefits you are receiving. This authenticity will be evident to others. They will begin to feel you are similar to them, and there is a relationship that has formed based on mutual interest.

You have the opportunity to choose the people with whom you want to associate. Not leaving the choice of friends to chance, you are systematically and deliberately laying the groundwork for friendship. Conversely, you are not leaving it to others to choose you. By making a decision as to the kind of people with whom you would like to associate, you are being proactive in nurturing friends. You are not simply waiting for them to find you, you are deciding the type of people by whom you want to be surrounded. Rather than leaving it to chance, make the chance and then take the chance.

TRANSFORMATION:

Don't wait for friends. Personally choose those you want to be your friends; then follow the steps to build relationships.

"Do not be misled: Bad company corrupts good character" (1 Corinthians 15:33)

By getting involved in several causes you feel passionate about, you are not only meeting others but enjoying yourself at the same time. You are bringing interest into your life in two ways. An interesting topic as well as interesting people are brought together as a result of choice and action. (1) You will be meeting others and satisfying an inner need to feel useful to society by volunteering for work in a service organization, and (2) you will be forging relationships and enjoying yourself by joining a hobby or special interest club.

A True Story

Judy was in her thirties with several children when her husband died in an automobile accident. Without warning, she was left alone with no close friends. How a person handles grief is a topic in itself. Any good book on handling grief will help you identify the steps in the grieving process.

Once Judy worked through the grieving process, she realized she had very few friends or relatives for support or with whom just to have fun. It's not that they had abandoned her intentionally. Afterward, she looked back and realized that all her friends had been married couples that she and her husband had chosen as companions. These married couples helped her through her husband's death and the immediate adjustment period, but she realized that as time went on, they felt awkward inviting her over by herself. They found it difficult to relate to her, a phenomenon many divorced single parents experience.

She craved friendships. Rather than to continue withdrawing and living with few outside interests, she decided to do something. She chose to widen her circle of association in several ways. First, she realized that this was the ideal time to finish her education. She had gone only briefly to college before getting married and having children. Now her children were a little older, and she had some funds from a modest life insurance policy that could cover the educational costs and help with child support for at least a few years. So she enrolled in college, first to complete general courses and then career-oriented courses.

She then began jogging again, a sport she and her husband had shared. Judy realized she had missed the stress relief and physical benefits this hobby had afforded, but not wanting to jog alone, she had discontinued her regimen. It was a good time to join a running club. The local sportswear shop put her in contact with several possibilities.

In a short time, Judy had made new friends. She was associating with others of like interest in a hobby she enjoyed. There were weekly gatherings for running with others and various events she attended with others. She also found acquaintances in her college classes that later became friends. She had not realized that many fellow students in college were in similar circumstances, having interrupted a quest for a college degree to work full-time or raise children. There were many other reentry students her age, older than the traditional college student.

Judy found new friends, friends with similar interests and similar goals, and in a similar age group. In fact, her new husband was a fellow student she met while completing her education. Judy again has many friends and a full life.

Networks

A powerful concept for success is networking which has been advocated as a means for making contacts and acquaintances to further your career. The idea is to meet people who can help you before you need them. Networking works just as well for friend-finding. The crucial ability required for either, though, is the ability to be genuinely interested in other people. Others can easily tell if you have a hidden agenda. They sense when an ulterior motive looms large in your mind. Be interested in other people. Each one has a unique story to tell, and you have the opportunity to learn from each. Practice caring about people.

Once you have developed a networking attitude, the next step is to acquire some of the social skills necessary for effective networking. There are many books on the market that can teach the rudiments of social networking. Many have been written from the standpoint of the effective use of networking for career, but the concepts are adaptable for use in social networking. Six basic skills are required:

(1) Be attentive when meeting others. Offer your hand to introduce yourself.

(2) Remember names. Many people say, "I can't remember names!" Often this is because they don't listen to others' names in the first place. They skip past another's name hoping to find out something important about them. Remember, though, to another person, what is important is his or her name. Make a conscious effort to remember people's names until it becomes a habit. Remind yourself that names are important. You will almost always remember a name simply by asking someone to repeat his name, consciously saying it aloud yourself and then using it once or twice in conversation. It's that simple. People are impressed when you care enough to remember their names. You can make it easier for others to remember your name by repeating it to them or suggesting how they might remember your name.

(3) Learn how to introduce yourself. Ahead of time, prepare a way of telling something about yourself in a few words so a new acquaintance becomes familiar with you immediately. In business networking, this means to explain in one or two sentences what you do and how you can be of help to them. In social networking it might mean relating how you happen to be in attendance. "I'm a relative of Bill, the host," or, "I've always been a model train enthusiast, and when I heard there was a local club, I couldn't wait to attend!"

(4) Learn how to attach yourself to a group of people already talking. Survey the room, looking for a group that is in need of having someone join. You normally can easily tell when several people are in intimate conversation or the level of animation is very high. These groups probably don't need your help, and you may feel like an intruder if you join an intimate conversation. However, there is usu-

ally at least one group where the energy level is low, and the group members are simply being cordial to others, making small talk. Here is where you can attach yourself to the group by walking up and giving your attention to the person speaking. When there is a break in the conversation, either introduce yourself or comment further on the topic of conversation. Remember, too, that a person standing alone usually will be grateful to have someone else approach.

(5) Learn to ask questions to draw others out. Ask questions that can't be answered by "yes" or "no." Questions such as, "How do you happen to be here today?" or, "How long have you known the hostess?" are usually enough to start a conversation and learn something about another. When going to a service organization, a simple question such as, "What draws you to this organization?" or, "How long have you been a member?" is a good conversation starter.

(6) Make a point to follow up with others. Whenever someone gives you helpful information or directs you to someone to contact, let the person helping you know how things worked out for you. This gives you a reason to keep in touch with a new friend. At the next gathering, make a point to express your appreciation or give her a call. Everyone likes to feel appreciated and to feel he or she has been of help. This will cement the relationship, too.

In this busy world, people seldom take the time to express their gratitude or make an effort to keep in contact. Any effort on your part is seen as an unexpected favor to others. Just a short note will serve the much-needed purpose of keeping in touch with others. Frequently we put off writing, thinking of the time it will take, but just a few moments are needed for a cordial acknowledgment. The stimulus might be a deserved compliment, a line of congratulations, or a word of thanks. All you need is a reason to write. This gesture is certain to cement a friendship, especially since any such gesture of thoughtfulness is uncommon in our high-tech, frantic-paced world. Your words of thanks or praise will surely be remembered and will stand out in an all-too-impersonal world.

A short note simply shows we care. One of the most famous note writers was President Abraham Lincoln. Among the most appreciated of his writings are the personal letters he wrote, some to strangers or brief acquaints. His letters of praise or condolences were cherished by the recipients and are still cherished to this day as national treasures. What made his notes so meaningful, and what will make ours so effective, is that they were short comments that expressed a sincere admiration for another's triumph over difficulty and tragedy or simply for another's success.

> **TRANSFORMATION:**
>
> *A personal interest in others is cherished in an impersonal world.*
>
> "Love your neighbor as yourself" (Matthew 22:39)

Meeting Checklist

When going to any gathering where you have the opportunity to meet people, people who you hope will become your friends, keep these things in mind:

(1) Realize that others will be nervous, so don't worry, you won't be the only one. Researchers have shown that 75 percent of people at any given social gathering will be uncomfortable. You will be no different from the majority.

(2) Go with a positive attitude. You might want to look at the gathering you're attending as a challenge to meet new people. Make it a goal to make three new contacts, three people you didn't know before who will become part of your ever-growing network of friends.

(3) Plan a short sentence to introduce yourself that tells others who you are and something about you, such as: "Hi, I'm Bill Williams. I'm from Detroit (your background),"

or "I'm a good friend of the groom (why you are there)." You may then want to ask others where they are from or their occupations. How they reply to your questions gives you a clue about how to continue.

(4) Prepare several ideas you might offer in small talk once you've met various individuals at the function. An experience you recently had, a topic in the news (if necessary, read the front page of the newspaper before you leave for the function), or something about a local sports team are all good conversation starters.

(5) Remember why you're going to the function. Your goal may be to make contacts or nurture an association with existing friends, or it may be to build support for your cause, or simply to meet others and enjoy yourself. Whatever the reason, clarify in your mind why you're going.

(6) Remember that conversation is like tennis, Ping-Pong, or other similar games. The object is to receive the ball and hit it back, trying to keep it in motion as long as possible. You don't hold onto it. In a good game of conversation you do the same. You listen or receive, and then you give or say something of interest, but then give the ball (the topic) back to the other person. Treat conversation as a game. Make it a challenge and have fun.

Reasons for Taking Time

The renowned research scientist, Hans Selye, stated that his guiding principle was to "earn the goodwill of others." A philosophy such as this reminds us that friendships need not initially require magnanimity on our part but only the desire to gain someone's attention or to coax others to care a little about us. Selye observed that collecting or hoarding is characteristic of all life just as egoism is. The goal of earning love is directed by this biological instinct. Selye considered the most useful and valued commodity that a person could collect was a bounty of goodwill which protects a person from personal attacks by others. Selye referred to his humanistic philosophy as "altruistic egoism." He observed that though a human is self-centered, he is motivated to collect the goodwill of others and to "amass an army of friends" as a survival mechanism. The way we accumulate the goodwill of others is to engender their love, gratitude, and respect by being indispensable to our neighbors. This philosophy of earning goodwill helps all that are involved in our circle of acquaintance and hurts no one. So if we have not acquired the habit of "loving our neighbors as ourselves" from a purely altruistic standpoint, we can at least begin to follow the philosophy with an egotistic reference to start. Either philosophy encourages us to gain personal satisfaction by helping others.

I state this philosophy to show that even from a purely biological standpoint the spiritual doctrine to "love thy neighbor as thyself" is founded on a scientific principle. Even if you don't yet have a spiritual outlook on life and don't see the connection of all things in this universe, you can recognize that the need to develop the goodwill of others is in everyone's best interest. Having a network of friends is a protection, but can be much more—it may be one of the very reasons for living! When you live by the goal of earning the goodwill of others, you make yourself indispensable to others and win their friendship. Earning the goodwill of others means doing things for others for which they will be grateful, and that means going out of your way for others.

The other related principle I stress here is the guideline of always working toward a *win-win* situation when dealing with others. If we act in a way that is in our best interest and is also in the other party's best interest, we build friendships. Over the years I've observed that nearly every negotiation can be structured in such a way that both sides come out ahead. This does not necessarily mean compromise, either. Merely a little extra initiative and energy must be expended, but the results are well worth the effort. Our own long-term best interest is served by being on good terms with others. We erect fewer barriers and make future situations more amenable to ourselves by following the principle of attempting to produce a *win-win* situation by our actions. Purely one-sided, selfish motives will cost us friends. Living by the *win-win* philosophy promotes friendship and the joy that comes from being with friends.

These two principles go hand-in-hand. Earning the goodwill of others means giving more than is expected of you. *Win-win* means taking an interest in others. Both ideas promote giving others what they need. Many times this simply means listening—*really* listening. What people want and desperately need is someone who will really listen to them, someone who is genuinely interested in their welfare. You need not be special in other ways, simply being special by standing out as someone who listens and really cares, cements a friendship. So often people ask in conversation, "How are you doing?" or, "How are you feeling?" and don't even await a reply. They show very little interest. As a result, most of us have learned to say when asked how we're doing, "Fine," even if it's not true. One way to stand out, but only if you mean it, when you know someone is *not* fine, and they answer with the perfunctory, "Fine," is to ask "How is it *really* going?" Others then realize you really do want to know, you really do care. So often that's what others need—someone to talk to. That's what friendship is all about. Take time with people and listen to what they have to say rather than just talking about yourself. Give others what they need and more than they expect.

> **TRANSFORMATION:**
>
> *Friendships are cemented by striving to earn the goodwill of others.*
>
> "The Golden Rule, attributed to Jesus, says: "Do unto others as you would have them do unto you" (Matthew 7:12 and Luke 6:31)

Activity

♦ Make a list of the people you are acquainted with and ask, "Who would I like to know better?" These may be acquaintances from work, groups to which you belong, such as civic or church groups, or they may be people you've met at social gatherings.

♦ If you don't have at least five or six names of potential new friends from this summary, follow the suggestions given above by resolving to join some group related to a hobby or special interest you presently have. Then resolve to follow the ideas previously presented on meeting people.

♦ Once you have decided on a list of potential friendship candidates, ask yourself how to go about making contact again. Which questions will you ask, or which statement will make you feel natural when calling?

These few steps will put you well on your way to expanding your network of friends.

Manners

A sadly neglected social skill needed for meeting and keeping friends is manners. Manners are not outdated. Since the pace of society is so feverish, and contact is so impersonal, manners are more essential than ever. Manners are essential for two reasons: (1) They are a way of impressing others (we all want to make good impressions), and (2) they put yourself and others at ease. When you know how you are expected to act and others do also, manners take uncertainty out of an encounter, allowing everyone more fully to be themselves.

Manners are much, much more than etiquette. Etiquette means rules of conduct, ways of behavior. Manners are a means of conveying good character and sending a message that you are respectful, kind and thoughtful. Manners tell others that you care, and they are essential for building friendships. You want to convey your thoughtfulness, your concern for others.

Most acts that indicate you are considerate of the other person would be examples of manners. Saying, "thank you," when treated kindly, repaying hospitality and generosity with like treatment, returning what is borrowed, and sincerely congratulating others on their accomplishments are examples of manners. In contrast, using what is considered profanity to some in public and refusing to return phone calls are examples of uncaring actions. Just because something is common practice does not justify its use. Profanity is frequently used in business and in public programming, but such improprieties still show a disregard to a good percentage of the population's sensitivities and thereby promote tension and ill ease. If you feel inadequate in this area, I suggest you get any book on manners from the library. Remember, the use of manners will make a good impression and put you and others at ease.

"Let your conversation be always full of grace, seasoned with salt, so that you may know how to answer everyone." (Colossians 4:6)

Power in Friends

I know someone who attributes her ability to handle the death of her mother without seriously destroying her equilibrium to her network of "dear friends," as she referred to them. Mary had always been especially close to her mother. In the last year her mother's health gradually faded, but the note of finality that death tolls is never easy to deal with, especially with a close companion. Mary admits she was just not prepared for the loss. She began to feel her control slipping away. Fortunately, Mary had close friends. One in particular, with whom she had gone to high school, was sensitive to her condition and immediately took time off to be with Mary and help pull her through the initial trauma. Mary had a husband who cared for her and children who appreciated her. However, her husband just couldn't project the necessary sensitivity, and Mary's children were too young to fully understand what she was going through. Looking back, Mary regards her friend's display of caring as one of her most cherished memories.

Mary had other friends, too. Almost immediately she was deluged with support. Friends from work called to console her. They assured her that her job responsibilities would be handled for as long as was necessary until Mary felt able to return. Friends from her church group volunteered to take turns making meals for the family, which allowed Mary time for grieving. The thoughtful cards and calls from friends from her bridge club were also welcomed comfort. Mary admitted she never realized how important her friends could be until she was forced to endure a personal tragedy. She said, "I've resolved to make myself available for support and consolation to my friends ever since I've experienced first-hand the indescribable treasure that close friends are."

Conversation

Finally, the founding of friendship is augmented by good conversation. Learning to converse well will beget friendship, and conversation doesn't mean talking to or at someone. Its goal is true communication, imparting of information. For this to occur requires:

(1) Time and leisure to engage in an unhurried discussion. Make a conscious effort to allot such time.

(2) Ability to express yourself freely without restriction of opinion or censure. Grant others the dignity of their opinions without immediate objections.

(3) Mutual attention. Give evidence you are personally interested in the conversation by leaning forward when the other party speaks, nodding to indicate understanding and interest.

(4) Working toward mutual self-disclosure. The willingness to reveal something about yourself is essential.

You are able to gauge the extent you actually had a conversation by the number of the above conditions present in the discussion. Considering friendship, I cannot stress enough the last of these requisites of conversation. To the extent you are willing to reveal yourself to others, others reciprocate and disclose something about themselves. Over time, as the disclosures become broader, as you reveal your true self by self-disclosure, your acquaintance becomes more familiar with you and is able to volunteer feelings and emotions previously hidden. This is how camaraderie and deep friendships are built. Practice cultivating the four above-mentioned conditions for good conversation, and assure yourself of creating lasting friendships.

Getting and keeping friendships requires effort. Keeping the lines of communication open does not occur by default. Keeping in contact demands the time to write or call or meet with friends. Good friendships are nurtured with hospitality, generosity, and the willingness to extend oneself for another, accommodating another even when that may mean inconvenience to you.

A good friendship also requires honesty. At times, it's easier to conveniently limit the truth, but maintaining intimacy may require effort to state the facts in such a way that you present the truth without judging and unduly injuring the other person. And then there's loyalty. At times, it would be easier not to stand by someone who is censured for committing an impropriety. Admitting we make our share of mistakes allows us to forgive and continue to think the best of our friends.

Is it any wonder close friendships are a rare commodity, and why most people can claim no more than two or three close

> **TRANSFORMATION:**
>
> *Set yourself apart by always dealing with others with honesty and loyalty.*
>
> "We are sure that we have a clear conscience and desire to live honorably in every way." (Hebrews 13:18)

friends? When we realize we have hundreds of contacts and acquaintances but maybe only enough friends that can be counted on the fingers of one hand, we're motivated to put forth the effort.

Friendship need not be such a rare commodity in life. We've talked about two types of friendships—friends as acquaintances (networks) and friends as close confidants. We need both, but I sincerely hope you experience your share of the beauty and sincerity of mutually close bonds.

"Think where man's glory most begins and ends
And say my glory was I had such friends." (William Butler Yeats)

CHAPTER 9

Creative Careers (Finance)

Although it was many years ago, I can still remember the exact moment and circumstance when I made the decision to make a deliberate career change. I was working as a janitor in the evenings when offices were closed. I didn't mind the manual work and didn't even mind the pay since it was perhaps a little above average. I remember so vividly, as I was putting away the buckets and mops one day, I declared emphatically, "I can't do this for the rest of my life. I've got to find a job that gives me a challenge! Besides, I have little children at home and another on the way. I don't want to be sleeping during the day while they're at school and working at night while they're home—I've got to make a change!"

I resolved at that moment I'd go into the insurance business. I had a friend in the business who had offered to hire me. Although he no longer was in insurance, I was sure I could find someone to give me a chance if I really proved I wanted to learn. I was also aware that I didn't need a college degree to begin. My resolve that day started the wheels in motion. It took months to research the steps that would be required and which company would be willing to take a chance on me since I had no experience. Eventually, I did find a company willing to hire me while I continued in my present job. It would be necessary to continue working as a janitor for some time, even part-time, to supplement my income until the commissions from sales were sufficient to live on.

I have never regretted that career change. It gave me the challenge I needed, the chance to grow and to use my abilities to a fuller extent. There may be a time when you have similar needs or, at least, you may want to reassess your present career path for potential. Here are some ideas I've found to be extremely helpful.

At least since the time of Martin Luther, Christians have recognized that one's calling could refer to more than just the *calling* to the priesthood or ministry. Any career or occupation could serve as a calling. "Whatever you do, work at it with all your heart, as working for the Lord." (Colossians 3:23) Recognizing that the average worker spends up to 50 percent of waking hours per week on the job, it's not difficult to see that your relationship with your job is a major determinant of your well-being. When admitting that your job is a major source of material security for yourself and family and a major influence on your self-concept, you are admitting that your career is a crucial concern, even if you would rather be pursuing other interests.

When a person is called *successful,* usually career success is being referred to. Since career growth, in most cases, will require more of your time than any other daytime activity, your attitudes, performance level, and enjoyment in your job largely define your sense of well-being. How could you be happy with your life if you are unhappy with an activity that will normally occupy over one-third of your waking hours? To the extent you are successful in your career, the tone for other aspects of your life will be set. We could say it's possible for one to be successful in one's career without success in life, but it's impossible to be successful in life without success in one's career. Being successful in your career means enjoying, performing well, gaining recognition, and feeling a sense of accomplishment in your work. This fact is well known, and perhaps this is why so much has been written on career-building and growth. Whether you are motivated to rise to the top of your field or desire a more fulfilling work experience, I'll provide you with ideas that will help you gain a sense of career well-being. One or two of these ideas are guaranteed to increase your pay 10-20 percent almost immediately once you adopt them!

Career success requires some specific habits and attitudes. I'll isolate several major outlooks and habits essential for whatever occupation you choose. These ingredients are critical. This practical advice will help you avoid time-consuming trial and error finding and then to progress in your chosen field.

As you embark on a new job or contemplate continuing in one you presently have, first ask yourself:

♦ Do I really enjoy the work?

♦ Have I ever compared the hours I spend on personal hobbies and leisure activities to the hours spent at work? (Most people find that the things they really enjoy occupy only a small fraction of the time spent on the job.)

♦ What if my work time were as enjoyable as the time allotted for hobbies?

Can you see where that in itself would provide you an edge over other employees or the competition?

If you enjoyed your job, it would not be drudgery to think about solving a problem or having to work a few hours overtime in an emergency. Observe the successful people you are aware of in any field. The trait that, more than any other, differentiates them is their love for their work. If they were billionaires and didn't have to work at their particular occupation, would they? That's the point—many of them *are* millionaires many times over—and even billionaires—but they continue working in the field because they enjoy it. Steven Jobs is a good example. He is one of the founders of Apple Computer, and it wasn't long after selling a controlling interest in his company that he was back in the field with a new venture. He enjoys working with computers, and that's precisely why he is so successful.

To get ahead in your career, ask yourself, "What do I love doing?" Then choose work in a field that allows you to do what you enjoy. If you are presently working in a

---

TRANSFORMATION:

Your career goal is to first find work you love to do.

"Whatever your hand finds to do, do it with all your might, for in the grave, where you are going, there is neither working nor planning nor knowledge nor wisdom." (Hebrews 13:18)

particular job, and perhaps have been for years, ask these two questions first:

♦ Do I love what I'm doing? If you're unable to respond *yes*, then ask,

♦ What aspect of my job do I love doing?

Once you know what you enjoy, you have several possibilities ahead of you. Ask:

♦ Can I spend more time in my present job doing that which I enjoy?

♦ Can I transfer to a different department in the same company that will allow me to devote more time to what I enjoy?

♦ Can I apply for work at a different company in my present field that will allow me to do more of what I enjoy?

Will it be necessary to make a career path change to find what you crave? Most people find they don't need to take such drastic action. If you presently believe striving for excellence in your present position is important, and you work to maintain a standard of excellence, you are probably already in a career position that is right for you—or at least one that has the possibilities to meet your need for enjoyment and employment simultaneously. If you think that your present position is worthy of your effort to strive for excellence, you no doubt already have that special affinity necessary for a successful career. You probably don't need to search for a new one since your attitude shows that you are in a career that is meaningful to you. For example, not everyone would have the inclination to put in the grueling training necessary to strive for excellence as an athlete unless he or she felt that it was worth the invested time and effort. The fact that an athlete willingly accepts what others would consider drudgery is an indication he or she is involved in a meaningful pursuit.

The major formula for career success is realizing what you enjoy doing (and there may be many possibilities here) and then setting your resolve to be the best there is at it. It's not complicated. It just takes time to decide and a firm resolve to follow through. Refer to Chapter 3 on goal-setting to formulate a plan. With this principle, you will be well on the way to career success.

Remember that what you enjoy doing is what you're probably good at. By finding work you enjoy, you are well on your way to distinguishing yourself in a career. You'll also enjoy your life more when you enjoy the work you do, and you'll find success comes with little effort.

Three Career Growth Rules

Once you have found a field of endeavor you can commit to and enjoy, there are steps you can take that will catapult you to the top of your profession. I have learned from experience and by observing career successes in various fields that there are three important rules to follow. These three attitudes, or resolves, will probably do more for promoting your success than any other. Furthermore, they're very simple:

(1) Treat yourself as a business.

Whether or not you embark on a career as an entrepreneur or business owner, treat yourself as just that. For example, if you work for a corporation, large or small, treat yourself as a business entity within that business—for you are indeed in the business of providing a service to the company for whom you work. It, in turn, is then providing a service to the public. This one attitude shift brings benefits far beyond the effort required. If you are a business, you are responsible. Getting the job done depends on you. You can't look to your supervisor or to your fellow workers for results; it depends on you. You can't wait for others to solve business problems; it's up to you! A business grows by providing a service better than others in its class. If you are to get ahead, you must think of yourself as such a business that is pro-

> **TRANSFORMATION:**
>
> *Treat yourself as a business within a business.*

viding a service that can't be matched by other businesses (other individuals) in its class.

Now follow this thinking through to its ramifications. Your position, if you are a computer programmer for a large corporation, is actually acting as a computer programming consultant for that corporation. As a consultant, the company you work for actually looks to you, not only to do the job but for advice and suggestions on how to improve its efficiency. Can you see how adopting such an attitude immediately puts you on a level above your peers, fellow employees in the company who are just doing the job they are being paid for but who have not taken this extra step? Furthermore, as a business owner, you, of "I, Inc." are willing to do more than the minimum to keep a customer happy since that customer will then buy from you in the future. You realize you want the company by which you are employed to continue buying your service and to continue paying more as your service becomes more complex, indispensable, and invaluable to them.

Your decision to treat yourself not as an employee, but as a business, immediately puts you in a different class from your peers. You offer something far more valuable than others. Whether you are a business consultant in the guise of an employee or in actuality are a small business owner opening a shop, you offer not only the product or service but also advice, suggestions, and the willingness to make it easy to do business with you. All this because you came to one simple realization: "I am a business and I, myself, am going to act as a business!"

(2) Commit yourself to becoming an expert in your field.

Being an expert makes the difference between being a highly valued company consultant or being just another employee. If you were having surgery, who would you want to do the operation? An expert in the field or just any doctor? If you needed some plumbing repairs done in your home, to whom would you rather offer the job, to an expert master plumber with a well-known reputation or to just any person who assures you he could do the job? How much more are you willing to pay for the expert? 10 percent more? 20 percent more? Can you see that your employer would also be willing to pay that differential or more if he regarded you as an expert in your field?

Whatever your field of endeavor, learn all you can about it. Read books on the subject, read current articles in trade journals on the subject, and inquire of others in the field for their experience and advice. In time, you will become the expert. Others will look to you for advice and aid. They will also be willing to accord you the recognition and financial compensation you deserve as a noted expert in the field. Again, the determinant is attitude, a simple shift in thinking: "I will no longer be just a computer programmer (a manufacturer's rep or designer), I will be an expert in my field. I will not go to others for help; one day they will come to me." That day will come, and it all starts with that simple decision you made: "I will be the best!"

(3) Find a niche.

Both large and small corporations are realizing that to survive in a competitive environment, they must carve out a niche and utilize their positions. All successful companies (Wal-Mart, Microsoft, and others) have a specific niche. They are not all things to all people. They have a specialized area of focus. This same philosophy can be applied by you in your own career. Find a niche—specialize. Make a specific, conscious decision that you will not just seek general knowledge in a particular field but that you will set your sights on one facet of that industry and know it extremely well. That's your niche, or area of specialization. A life insurance salesman may specialize in working with small, closely-held corporations, for example. Her vast experience and specialized knowledge will allow her to offer her clients advice that the ordinary

> **TRANSFORMATION:**
> *Career success requires finding a niche in your industry or company and specializing. Back to "I, Inc".*

generalist would be unable to match. The satisfaction that comes from doing what few others can do and the monetary compensation received transform an ordinary career into an enjoyable labor.

Here is where your initiative and creativity come into play. For example, on which area of expertise as a manager could you focus? Human resources management? What about decision-making? There are many specialized aspects to pursue. What can you do or could you do better than anyone in the industry, or at least in your company? It stands to reason you will be better compensated, and you'll enjoy your occupation that much more.

I know a residential home builder (there are hundreds in the area) who specializes in building energy-efficient homes, and because of this, he has gained a reputation that differentiates him from the crowd. I have been assisted by customer service representatives in various companies who are so well-versed in the application of their product that they earned my patronage and admiration. They are indispensable to their firms. They know it, and their superiors know it.

Find that area of expertise, something within your chosen field, something you truly enjoy doing. The satisfaction gained from feeling indispensable can't be matched!

In summary, the three career decisions that will yield profound results are:

- ◆ Act as if you run your career as a business
- ◆ Find a specialization in your field
- ◆ Become an expert in that field

Once these three principles of attitude are indelibly impressed on your psyche, the ingredients for a successful career do not vary much by field of endeavor. There are four specific ingredients common to most career success surveys I've analyzed. They are:

- ◆ Set very specific goals and monitor results regularly.
- ◆ Work on the mastery of time organization.
- ◆ Continue acquiring specialized knowledge in your field.
- ◆ Work on maintaining prosperous and optimistic business attitudes.

These themes invariably appear in the lives of successful people in every field.

A successful company maintains its position and growth by giving attention to all the major aspects of its operation. The prosperous enterprise has a system for manufacturing (or service), a system for marketing and accounting, a provision for research and development, and an overall management system. A business will remain successful only if all these systems are operational. If marketing efforts begin to falter, if the feedback accounting systems are not maintained, or if the company makes no provision for future competitive position through research and development, the company soon begins to flounder and falter.

In much the same way, you must manage your career. Give attention to making yourself valuable to your employer, be that employer a customer or a superior. First have the assurance within you that you have something of great value that can be offered to others, but then make certain to advertise or market your skills subtly to be sure others recognize their value. In no aspect is a career-oriented person more conspicuous than in her continual insistence on investing in herself. Money or time can never be spared when it comes to improving your innate worth as a person and as a business enterprise. The time and money for education are of no object because they are investments in yourself. You'll never hesitate making an investment required for proper equipment or improved skills to do your job better. Investing in yourself is the surest investment possible. Dividends are returned many times over.

Personal management requires something else. A good business is well-organized and uses its accounting system not so much to keep track of profits but as a feedback mechanism. Since the business is concerned about staying focused and maintaining its competitive advantage, it uses feedback systems to track its performance fluctuation. Most successful individuals admit that they use their income in much the same way. A growing income is considered an indicator of one's increasing value to society more than as a gauge for increasing wealth. In Chapter 3 on goals, we covered the importance of having precise, measurable goals as a means to track our progress and maintain our direction. Most successful people, as the successful businesses they are, consider it essential to track progress in all aspects of their multi-faceted operations as a business enterprise.

The main factor that differentiates the successful person from those of negligible achievement is his motive for being in business. A successful entrepreneur is motivated more by an idea than by money, and is excited to see an idea become reality. The sheer pleasure that comes from taking a unique concept and working with it until it materializes is the real motivator. Certainly money is important, but the entrepreneur believes if there is a good concept and a sound strategy, the money for implementation and reward will follow. The primary focus is never merely on profits but on implementation of ideas. The entrepreneur recognizes that once money is made the focus, attention shifts from the factors that initially made success possible. You are such an entrepreneur whether you own your own business or are employed as a business within a business.

If you are employed by another company, you need a sustaining business philosophy. Outstanding service to others is one such philosophy. Production of a superior product might be another. A desire to be of superior service, for example, is commensurate with the level of compensation. The two are inseparable. My studies over the years of motives for business success have convinced me that rarely is a successful businessperson motivated only by level of service *or* level of compensation. Invariably it is a combination of the two. This is similar to your motive for doing a favor for a friend. Why do you act? That's difficult to answer. You do the favor, perhaps because you feel an obligation or a duty, but you also are motivated by the good feeling you have for acting simply because he or she is a friend, not expecting any reciprocation. Similarly business motives are not so easily dissected into simple components. The successful businessperson desires material rewards for services rendered but also is motivated by feeling indispensable to others. The two motives are inextricably linked.

> ### TRANSFORMATION:
>
> *The motivation for career growth is always more than the material rewards; it's the desire to provide ever-improving services or products.*
>
> "To be rich in good deeds, and to be generous and willing to share" (1 Timothy 6:18)

One day the major inducement for your extra attention to business may be personal gain, but the next day it may be a genuine desire to help others and to demonstrate a concern for others' welfare by offering outstanding services or products. While there is no reason to deny the motive of personal gain since we share with all living organisms the selfish survival mechanism built within us, that self-centered mechanism cannot sustain long-term excitement. Something else is required. As your need for self-gain and fulfillment are satisfied, you naturally gravitate toward the more altruistic motive of feeling useful to others. This higher motive becomes a sustaining force.

Personal Management

In giving direction on career paths I always go back to the attributes of effective managers. I have stressed the idea that our personal business careers must be run as small businesses. Since the backbone of any business is management, emulate the qualities of a good manager as you build your career. Superior managers reveal the following common attributes. They:

♦ Seek out and accept responsibility

♦ Are goal driven

♦ Display total commitment to the task

♦ Practice superior communication skills

♦ Evince a caring attitude toward others

♦ Help others grow by delegating tasks

These are attitudes and attributes suitable for business and, therefore, suitable for managing your personal career growth. Management skills are required first to manage yourself but also, as you grow in your own organization as an entrepreneur or as an employee manager in a large firm, to manage others. You might ask yourself, "Which of these management attitudes do I now exhibit? Which can I improve ?"

Several General Principles

I have not given specific advice on career growth. Since each industry has a somewhat different career path, I've suggested general rules. Though general, they are perhaps the most important element in success. Here are two more related general pieces of advice that will serve you well. First, whatever your field of endeavor, look around at those who are already successful in that career. Study their actions and emulate their habits. It stands to reason that if they are in positions you admire, you can do the things they did to produce similar results in your career. Imitate their habits. This advice holds true for any career path. Look for the successful, then emulate their habits and attitudes. They are living career manuals, and easily observable. They can act as your mentors without knowing it.

One corollary to this principle of imitation applies to appearance. The cardinal rule in corporate America and in small business is to follow the leader. Your appearance communicates a great deal about you. Some of what you communicate is not what you may intend. If you wish to acquire responsibility in a large corporation, be sure your appearance suggests you are capable of that responsibility. Follow the leader. Dress as he or she does. If you wish to succeed in small business, also follow the leaders in that niche market. Dress as they do. Identify the image you wish to project and dress accordingly. For example, I talked to one insurance agency executive who told me that since he deals with smaller contractors all day long, many of whom come from the work sites, he dresses to project the image of being successful while at the same time not being intimidating to them. In his case, this means driving a late model top-of-the-line car like an Oldsmobile rather than a Mercedes or BMW. It also means dressing in sports coats rather than executive suits. He identified the image he wished to project and made the necessary adjustments. Though he could easily have afforded any automobile and any designer suits he wished, he realized image was more important.

Career Networking

In the last few years, *networking* has been stressed as a major key to career success. Networking is collecting and using contacts with other individuals in a wide variety of circles, including not only businesses related to your field but also service organizations, and political and social groups. Consulting with others can provide a fresh perspective not only when problems arise but to avoid potential problems. Hearing firsthand experiences dealing with marketing, employee compensation, and fighting international competition can provide solutions that can prove invaluable to you in the future. Often just hearing about an innovative approach taken to solve a problem is the most valuable benefit of networking, though many shortsightedly use their contacts solely for prospective sales leads or for new job offer contacts.

> **TRANSFORMATION:**
>
> *Career networking only works if you are determined to be of mutual benefit to others.*
>
> "Do nothing out of selfish ambition or vain conceit"
> (Philippians 2:3)

Networking is a continual process of meeting and keeping in contact with others to whom you can be of potential benefit and to whom you can turn for assistance. There are many good books on the subject—especially since it is a current hot topic. Consulting any of these texts will give you a list of possibilities that will jog your memory of past associates and acquaintances to add to your collection of available resources. You will also get advice on how to keep in touch with these contacts. But the basic philosophy behind networking is being of mutual benefit to others. This requires a commitment to look for ways you can be of assistance to others, providing them with advice, referrals, suggestions and, in general, giving of your time. Giving of your own resources without seeking an immediate payback is the only way a network will work. Reciprocal dealings with others provide you with the satisfaction of helping others while allowing you the privilege of asking for help when that becomes necessary. Many successes in the top of their respective fields have attributed their achievement directly to their ability to maintain useful contacts.

Career Burn-Out

Finally, success in any endeavor means persistence. Unfortunately, one of the major causes of career casualty is job burn-out. A successful career requires continual enjoyment of work activities. It's only after years in a business that you begin to reap the benefits of your experience, contacts, and knowledge. If you are forced to leave an industry just when you are beginning to see the rewards for your investment of time, what a waste of precious years! Three major causes of job burn-out I've observed over my years of my involvement in business activities are:

♦ Suitable Activities

♦ Outlook

♦ People Skills

We need to find *suitable activities* in the type of work that we enjoy doing and in which we have competence. This requires acknowledging, "This is what I have chosen as my career. I have not been coerced into this position. The skills required to succeed at this position are ones that I already have or that I can acquire without difficulty. I see a value and purpose to the work I do." Making this assessment will assure you that there is no basic reason why you should ever have to suffer burn-out. If this inventory cannot be answered to your satisfaction, you may need to consider initiating simple minor changes, such as transferring to a different department or, if in sales, soliciting to a more specialized market niche to restore your contentment. Major adjustments are seldom needed and should never be committed to without a great deal of meditation and cost-counting. However, when you have to take drastic measures, take solace by recognizing that future inevitable difficulties have been circumvented by foresight in the present.

Frequently the difference between job satisfaction or discontent is simply a matter of minor adjustments in our *outlook*. You may not be able to change the environment but you can change the way you respond. This too requires a conscious effort. Start by acknowledging, "I cannot do everything myself. I have limitations. I may never be able to do certain things extremely well, but there are always resources available to help me accomplish a task." Acknowledging your limitations helps you to delegate or share responsibilities, and that immediately alleviates pressure.

Work to cultivate an outlook that allows you to see the good that comes from your job. For example, what is a carpenter doing? Is he just pounding nails, or is he building a house that will be the dream home for some fortunate family? Outlook is important. As an encyclopedia salesman, are you selling just to make a living, or are you helping parents fulfill their wishes to give their children the resources that will provide for academic success? In any occupation, there is a need to acquire an outlook that sustains your career. I adamantly believe that nearly any job can be reconstructed mentally into a positive contribution to humanity.

Efforts that don't work out can be viewed either as failures or as successful identification of possibilities that don't work. It's all in the way you perceive a situation. Make an effort to at least acknowledge to yourself that the negative is not the only way to look at the frustrating outcome. Ask, "What is the good that can come from this seeming failure? Have I possibly avoided future, more serious difficulties by identifying presently an option that was not workable? Have I learned something useful from this failure?" Salvaging something useful from the mishap changes the seeming failure to an outright success!

Finally, people with fulfilling lives are always willing to equate possibility with hope. When there is a possibility that the next project attempted will work, immediately there is hope. This hope then can sustain us in the interim until at least a modicum of success appears.

Honing our *people skills* will also help avoid burn-out. I find the one major disability potential burn-out candidates have is the inability to say "no." Always acceding to pleas for help leads, in time, to stress and resentment. Some never can admit that the reason they cannot say "no" is out of fear that others will dislike them. They don't seem to realize that an acquaintance who will dislike us merely because we wouldn't help them at that particular moment is not the kind of associate we want anyway. Besides, the people whose solicitations we decline will soon forget they had ever asked us. Learning to say "no" immediately to any project that is not a valuable use of your time or that does not hold any real interest to you is a necessary people skill. Learning to say, "That's a worthwhile project, but I know I could not do it justice due to my time schedule and my prior commitments," is simple and eliminates resentment.

Learning to assign projects to others is another necessary people skill. This may first require admitting either someone else can do a better job or that, on a non-critical assignment, someone else can do the job almost as well as you. Countless articles are written about how delegation enhances both the career of the delegator and delegatee. This is another of those *win-win* situations. Assigning responsibility gives us the credit for getting the job done, frees up time for other essential tasks, while permitting another to learn a new skill and prepare for future, more complex assignments.

Acquiring the habit of seeing the good qualities and abilities in our subordinates and peers and then complimenting them on their efforts is an extremely important people skill. This propensity to see good and to spread enthusiastic praise has a reciprocal effect on us.

These are but a few examples of people skills useful in avoiding burn-out. There are others, of course, but enough has been said to alert you to this possible remedy to potential job burn-out.

Activity

♦ Prepare a job resume. Even if you have no plans to make a job change, a resume will remind you of the skills you have acquired that might be better utilized in your present position.

♦ If you realize you may need to re-market yourself, go to the library and get a book on resume writing to provide you with the most effective format for presenting yourself.

♦ In either case, pay particular attention to the abilities you have demonstrated in past job positions. What are they?

♦ Also list your accomplishments in school (e.g. student council), volunteer work, and your hobbies, in addition to on-the-job projects completed.

♦ You should realize you have a lot to offer your present and future employers. With the experience you've had, there is every reason you will succeed in your career.

Here's to Your Career

We have come full circle, covering launching a career and maintaining one. You will find other useful career-related information in Chapter 3 on goal attainment, problem-solving, and personal relationships. Later, Chapter 12, "The Secret of Balance," will help with a major problem many successful people encounter—keeping priorities straight and integrating the time required to maintain a successful career with the time necessary to enjoy the other aspects of life. Finally, Chapter 11, "Dominant

Dreams (Fame)" goes into great detail on how to integrate your hobby into your career path, and that may be one of the greatest aids to your career growth.

I wish you one of the most considerate thoughts I could ever offer, that you enjoy a prosperous career and a sense of continued career growth and satisfaction.

"In order that people may be happy in their work, these three things are needed: They must be fit for it. They must not do too much of it. And they must have a sense of success in it." (John Ruskin)

"Whatever you do, work at it with all your heart, as working for the Lord, not for men." (Colossians 3:23)

CHAPTER 10

Essential Education (Faculties)

Have you ever thought of the most embarrassing moment you ever endured? For me, I guess I'd have to say it was back in high school. I was a shy, reticent student. One day while I was in the library, one of the most popular girls in school smiled and motioned in my direction. I didn't know how to react. Why would someone that popular smile at *me?* First I responded with a feeble smile, then she beckoned again. I mustered the courage to start walking in that direction. When I was almost there, she started talking. Only then did I realize she was smiling and beckoning to another student, not me! I was mortified. I didn't know how to react. I wanted to sink into the cracks! How could I have been so silly to even think that she would ever speak to me? I just sort of slithered away inconspicuously.

I mention this to underscore the fact that education is multi-faceted. In high school I was a good student. I was taught analytical geometry and calculus, but my education woefully neglected training in the areas of character development and social skills. Not till I got out of high school did I recognize that if I were to succeed I'd have to gain an education in these areas, too. I began to realize what I hope you have already come to realize—education includes not just training for careers, but also for social skills and personal growth, and education can never be discontinued unless you want to be rendered obsolete in our society.

Ever since the Bible became available to the common man with the invention of the printing press, education has held a prominent place in the Judeo-Christian world. In general, statistics have shown that the literacy rate of Christian countries in the past has been far higher than that of non-Christian countries. The special envoys of God and the Kings of Israel were instructed to "...write for himself on a scroll a copy of this law...and is to read it all the days of his life." (Deuteronomy 17:18-19) Note that the idea of life-long learning is introduced here. Even to this day, many Christians make it a resolve to daily read the Bible for personal edification. Spiritual growth is of paramount importance, but what about growth in other areas and continuing education in general? What I advocate here is that you commit to life-long learning in all aspects of life.

Education includes the perfecting of your abilities, your competence, and your personal resources. If you want to function at your optimum, your attributes and knowledge must not remain stagnant over time. Though your formative years produce the most noticeable increases in personal competence, as a fully functioning individual, your personal faculties are expected to continually improve. This is a far-reaching commitment. Consider for a moment all the areas into which your education permeates. As you grew physically, you were expected to grow in mental ability, in emotional stability, in social adjustment, and in general knowledge with the expectation you would become a self-sufficient, fully functioning member of society. I am going to provide you with a simple plan for continuing education and growth. Following this plan will give you a sense of competence and well-being. You'll never feel obsolete.

As you grew up, society expected you to be constantly improving your character and abilities. When you reached adulthood, this expectation of growth suddenly was no longer stressed. You were no longer expected to continue making progress. Studies have found that the majority of college graduates have not read a complete book other than a novel in the five years since graduation! When asked why, many will say they felt all the years invested in education were sufficient. However, the world is changing, our environment is evolving, so logically our skills and knowledge need to continue to keep up with our dynamic world. Out of necessity, and for your continued happiness, education must be a never-ending pursuit.

When I speak of education I am talking about the training and perfecting of all your human faculties. The skillful use of faculties must include not only your mental and intellectual capabilities but also your social skills and professional skills. Your emotional and psychological faculties must grow as well.

Schools tend to focus only on the one area of intellectual progress. However, knowledge has limited usefulness if, as we acquire it, our other faculties have not kept pace. How could we employ or even communicate new ideas if the required social skills to interact with and persuade others are lacking? Competence in intellectual, emotional (psychological), and social skills produces a fully functioning individual and opens the door to many opportunities.

Looking-Glass Self

We have a need to know our abilities and have confidence in them if we are to use them effectively. Two major concepts in social psychology are a help in understanding this. They are referred to as *The Looking Glass Self* and *The Self-fulfilling Prophecy*. Each idea has been substantiated time and again by rigorous research studies. Together they prove that your *self-concept* is one of the most powerful forces at work and will have a major impact on the outcome of any endeavor you undertake. By *self-concept* I am referring to the basic opinion you have about yourself, your talents, abilities, and worth as an individual. If you possess a positive self-concept, you enjoy a feeling of inner self-worth and, as a result, trust yourself and your abilities. The important point to remember is that you are not born with a self-concept—you develop one over time.

The Looking Glass Self, first proposed by Charles Horton Cooley during the early part of this century and frequently supported since then, tells us that the *self* develops based on how we think our talents and behavior appear to others, how we think others judge our talents and behavior, and then how we feel about their judgments. We imagine how we appear to others and how they evaluate our appearance and abilities. Whether our ideas about ourselves are accurate or not, we believe them. We then respond to these imagined evaluations of ourselves with feelings of pride and confidence or self-disapproval and inadequacy. The point is, we make the evaluation. We see ourselves as if in a looking glass. That looking glass is society. As we interact with others, we see reflected back to us an image of ourselves and accept this image as being an accurate picture of who we truly are. Unfortunately, we often estimate our self-worth as being far less than it is.

Self-Fulfilling Prophecy

A serious consequence of this *Looking Glass Self* is the *Self-fulfilling Prophecy*, developed years ago by Robert Merton and verified by the startling results of psychological studies. A *Self-fulfilling Prophecy* is a prediction we make that causes us to act as if that prediction were true, and, as a result, it comes to pass because of our own actions. This is especially true with our predictions about ourselves. If we hold a particular definition of ourselves to be true, we will act as if it were true, and as a result it comes true. For example, if I believe I am a confident, self-assured person, I will act that way. As a result, others will treat me accordingly and their treatment of me will reinforce my assessment of myself. It makes no difference if the original definition of myself were true or not. I act according to the definition I hold to be true, and as a result it becomes true.

For you to feel good about yourself then, you must first be convinced at least of the potential of your own ability and worth as a person. As you perfect your talents and abilities and see the progress in your own life, you develop confidence that enables you to attempt greater projects. Personal growth is critical. As you progress in education and perfecting of your talents, you accept your abilities and begin to trust them. You then become convinced of your self-worth. As a result, more and greater projects are attempted and successfully completed. All this is based on your original assessment of your abilities.

This cycle works with our mental faculties, our emotional constitution, and our social abilities. As we make a concentrated effort to develop our talents and use them, we become convinced

TRANSFORMATION:

Our self-concept becomes a self-fulfilling prophecy.

"According to your faith will it be done to you." (Matthew 9:29)

of our abilities and develop confidence in them. As this confidence grows, we're more willing to use our talents, and finally the outcome we seek and predict will manifest itself. Only by consciously and methodically working on our attributes and talents will we be aware of them and begin to trust them and, therefore, use them. As we perfect them, these talents blossom and naturally produce greater accomplishments in our lives.

Intellectual Wonder

I encourage you to cultivate a sense of wonder about yourself, about your abilities, about the world around you, and about the marvels of life. With such an outlook, you'll experience a desire to learn, to understand, and to nurture your intelligence.

Intelligence is the ability to make sense of the world. This "making sense" requires organizing what is learned into a useful form and then using it to adapt to this world. An intellectual endeavor then is the process of:

♦ Organizing new information

♦ Integrating it with what we already know

♦ Using this new information to adapt to or manipulate the world around us

The goal is to come continually to more efficient concepts of the reality or realities around us. The closer our mental concept is to the actual pattern of the environment around us, the more readily and successfully we are able to adapt to this environment and perhaps to transform it. We strive intellectually to come to an ever-improving understanding of life and as that life changes or evolves, to discern these changes and nuances. This is a never-ending process.

The goal of intelligence, then, is not the accumulation of random and miscellaneous information. We are bombarded with data from all sides. Our society has produced information overload, more information than could possibly be absorbed and used by anyone. Much of the information is trivial and of minimal value. Our goal is not to indiscriminately absorb these data but to rummage through them, to ferret out the helpful data and to organize them into a usable form. This is *now* knowledge. A person can be well-informed and at the same time hopelessly ignorant! Information is expanding so rapidly that we're being inundated and overwhelmed by it. You might say we are in danger of being drowned by information. Focus is necessary, a realization that this miscellaneous information must be organized in a form that can be put to work. Our intellectual faculties attempt to do this.

We can all relate to this by thinking of the room, garage, or desk drawer most of us have at home, where we just throw things to get them out of the way, reasoning we might use them some day. As you know, we seldom use those materials since it would take forever to rummage through everything to find what is wanted. The problem is these things are not organized and easily retrieved. This is much the same with new information we acquire. If we don't apply the data immediately to what we already know, or write it down, or put it in a file that logically links related information, the chances of our ever using the data are negligible.

One of the first steps is to develop, if we don't already possess it, this sense of wonder toward life and the world around us I just mentioned. Our desire needs to be to exhibit continually the enthusiasm of a young child. Children are continually entranced by beauty, by oddity, and by new sights, never treating them as banal or uninteresting. Unfortunately, as adults age, we tend to lose that exhilaration or surprise that comes from learning something new. So common is this loss that a person's age can frequently be gauged by the level of interest one manifests in the surrounding world. The task is to make the effort to retain the sense of wonder toward life, to reject the foolish notion that learning is merely for young children. None of us can afford mental stagnation if we are to continue really living. Rather than be stifled by fixed habits and routines, we need to learn new ways of viewing and reacting to our world. We can choose whether to treat ourselves as our own mental prisoner. To the extent we make an effort to acquire knowledge and to further organize it into understanding and use it as wisdom, we break through the mental jail cells that inhibit us.

Learning, then, is much more than simply taking in data. It includes observation and then practical application to ourselves. We learn to accept other people as they are; we learn to trust our instincts; we learn to accept the fact we will never be well thought of by everyone and, therefore, need not be influenced by their whims and tastes. This learning builds to provide a firm foundation for living. Eventually our quest for understanding provides meaning and direction to life!

A Road Map for Learning

To do well in the pursuit of knowledge and understanding, it helps to have a plan for learning. Setting up an organized program for reading is a good first step. This plan for reading might include provisions to gain general knowledge regularly and to learn more about your chosen career and to pursue special fields of interest. Both types of knowledge are needed—generalized knowledge of the world, including the learning of skills for successful living, and specialized knowledge of our chosen area of concentration, including both vocational and avocational knowledge. The goal is to become:

♦ An expert in living

♦ An expert in at least one specialized field of knowledge

This goal of being a *life expert* requires reading books and journals that help us acquire the skills that allow for a successful life. As problems arise in life, you may choose to do research at the library or a local bookstore to find personal help on dealing successfully with a particular personal problem. On the other hand, a regular reading program in your career and avocational field will allow you to stay abreast of the newest information in your field. You will have cutting-edge information updated for current use.

Activity

What I am advocating is an organized program for the progressive attainment of focused knowledge. Read and study with specific goals in mind. I propose that your reading program include three areas:

♦ Keep abreast of current events in our changing world perhaps by reading a weekly news magazine.

♦ Build living skills-social skills, such as conversing and relating to other people, and mental health skills, such as maintaining a healthy psychological outlook.

♦ Maintain knowledge and skills in a chosen career field that excites you. That excitement is the motivation to get you to read progressively the seminal books in that field.

To succeed in this ambitious program of knowledge attainment will require a plan. Time must be set aside daily, if possible, for reading. Many busy people find that setting time the first thing in the morning or the last thing at night works well. Set aside a specific time and a specific amount of time. Form a habit so that nothing is allowed to interfere with this priority time. Then follow an organized plan of reading with specific goals in mind. Your

TRANSFORMATION:

Begin a life-long education project that will prepare you to take advangtage of opportunities as they arise.

"And he is to read it all the days of his life so that he may learn to revere the Lord his God and follow carefully all the words of this law and these decrees." (Deuteronomy 17:19)

efforts in a short time will allow you to feel you are one of the competent members of society with a broad background of knowledge providing the necessary wisdom to succeed in both career and personal life. Imagine how your self-confidence will soar as you master these ideas.

Living Skills

As important as intellectual exercise is to gaining competence in living, so also is the attainment of interpersonal skills. Several of these skills have already been introduced as fostering intellectual growth. Three skills are among those stressed most often in self-help groups and self-improvement literature over the last thirty years:

- ◆ Holding onto a childlike wonder and willingness to learn

- ◆ Displaying self-confidence

- ◆ Maintaining an assertive attitude

You will be able to find abundant, detailed material on any of these through a search of the self-improvement literature. My goal here is to affirm the importance of each and to stress that these and other such skills can be acquired and maintained through an organized program of study and practice similar to the program for intellectual and career fulfillment I have already described. All aspects of personality can be changed. You need only identify the area where improvement is needed and systematically practice a trait until it becomes second nature.

The Child Within

Holding a childlike attitude toward others and toward life is essential for fulfillment. I've already mentioned that this attitude includes a desire to learn and a tendency to be in wonder at the knowledge and experience that life has to offer. The quality is also a major source of satisfying interpersonal relationships. A childlike attitude ingratiates us to others and simultaneously allows us to be accepting of others. Children are excited about new experiences and look on them as adventures. Adults, too, can be just as excited about meeting new people. Every new person, every new interpersonal encounter can be a welcomed occasion to learn, to be entertained and transfixed by the personal experience of others. "Childlike" also describes a person who is non-judgmental, forgiving, and unprejudiced toward others. Strive to be genuine, unsophisticated, and down-to-earth, which are all aspects of the spirit of a child. Interestingly, these are also the bases for good communication. Being childlike guards against cynicism and, in turn, provides for self-renewal of the spirit. "Become as little children," Jesus, the master teacher, said. (Matthew 18:3)

How do we do this? It's really one of the easiest skills to master since we have all at one time experienced the delights of this way of life. It's just necessary to recall and relive the experience. Think how great a glass of water tasted after you ran home; how sweet the smell of freshly cut grass; how magical the twinkling of fireflies on a warm summer night. Remember the wonder you felt when being introduced to new experiences. Then be determined to again feel this way regularly.

> **TRANSFORMATION:**
>
> *Make a conscious effort to regain the joy and wonder of learning new things you had as a a child.*
>
> "Let the little children come to me, and do not hinder them, for the kingdom of God belongs to such as these. I tell you the truth, anyone who will not receive the kingdom of God like a little child will never enter it." (Luke 18:16,17)

Realizing you may have lost something beautiful, a precious treasure, will help you get the feeling back. The sheer joy of that past time in your life will motivate you to desire its return. Just remember and act accordingly. Once you get in touch with this sense of wonder you once had about life, you'll never want to misplace it again!

Self-Confidence

I've already mentioned that the learned quality of self-confidence is a major interpersonal skill necessary for growth. That's *learned* self-confidence. I have found this attitude can be acquired by making the effort to program ourselves with positive thoughts:

♦ Emphasize the good qualities and abilities you have.

♦ One by one, work to improve the skills at which you may not be as accomplished.

♦ As you make this effort, you naturally begin to feel positive about yourself.

♦ Then as you begin, at first reluctantly and tentatively, to step into unfamiliar and perhaps fearful circumstances, you gain the confidence to attempt further challenges that may have been fear-inspiring in the past.

The point is this: Don't wait until you feel no fear before trying something new, but try it in spite of discomfort. As you attempt these hitherto fearful tasks, your discomfort diminishes, and you expand your *comfort zone* to include a wider range of activities. Cultivate the attitude, "I'm afraid, so what?" Every person alive has some fears, some more than others, but as you attempt what you fear, starting with the little things, you build up the strength to attempt a more difficult feat the next time. This is how I approach going into the water at the beach. The water may be cold, but I know if I don't take a step at a time, though it's uncomfortable, I'll never go swimming. I've learned I must be willing to put up with the discomfort first with my feet, then my legs, until I am submerged and acclimated to the change in temperature. Let's apply this same lesson to venturing out into life.

You can never eliminate all fear but you can *control* fear. Don't allow it to manage you; make the effort, even forcing yourself at first, to manage it. Also, don't berate yourself for being fearful. Control of fear is a lifelong process that every individual must confront on a regular basis. There is not one person who is not afraid or apprehensive about some new situation in some facet of life. The self-confident are the ones who nudge themselves to act in spite of fear and find that as their *comfort zone* expands, there is one less fearful situation to worry about.

Often fear elimination is simply a matter of admitting, "Yes, I am fearful." This is the first step. Confronting the fear means being observant when fear arises. Then analyze, "Why am I experiencing fear?" I found in my own life that these fears were consistently based on some underlying fears—the fear of conflict and the fear of displeasing others. Once I dissected my fears into its component parts, they became much easier to handle. I've recognized that for me, fear of conflict was founded on my childhood experience of always coming out on the short end of a disagreement with my parents or other elders. I formed the habit of fearing and avoiding conflict as a means of self-preservation. I have realized, though, I am no longer a helpless child, and I have far more options to choose from as an adult in dealing with conflict. I need no longer habitually use fear (which to me, in many cases, is just conflict-avoidance) as a major coping technique.

I recognized also that my fear of displeasing others and desiring to be well thought of also was a formed habit. Coming from a relatively poor economic background and thinking I might not be as capable as others forced me to fight to gain the approval of others and to fear displeasing them. Again, as an adult, I have realized I don't need to continue carrying this burden. So at first I tried tentatively and then, in time, more boldly to attempt what I feared. I remember the first few times I started a new business venture. The fear of failure was intense. I kept catching myself thinking negatively about the outcome. I had to force myself to just keep doing what I knew had to be done if I were ever to succeed. I proved to myself what independent studies have borne out—that 90 percent of our fears never even materialize. Think of it, nine out of ten of your fears will never come to pass! Using this statistic, some have confronted fear by simply asking, "What is the worst that can result from this step? Could I survive this *worst case scenario?*" If the answer to that last question is yes, and since nine out of ten times it won't happen anyway, why not take the chance? This exercise of your will, like any exercise program, allows you to feel more capable over time. Mental exercise, like physical exercise, requires repetition to show results. In time, confrontation of fear and exercising our will produce an increasing level of self-confidence, an invaluable interpersonal skill.

Assertiveness is Not an Extreme

Another important skill is assertiveness. Assertiveness is not aggression. Aggression promotes conflict, while assertiveness promotes expressing yourself openly and honestly. By working at being assertive, you increase your communication skills and demonstrate a willingness to negotiate if necessary. An assertive person wants to express her feelings, ideas, or opinions but also is willing to allow others to express their views.

When adequate communication is attained, everyone in the discussion benefits. This is the desired result, and assertiveness allows for it. Unfortunately, some never reach this point of clear communication, remaining at the personality extremes of aggressiveness or shyness (reticence to express oneself). These extremes can usually be lessened by first recognizing the desirability of open communication and realizing these extremes block the desired goal.

An aggressive person makes it more difficult for others to accede to his wishes. He erects barriers to the attainment of his own goals. If his goal is to have someone act on his behalf, this is more easily accomplished without applying extreme force, and the respondent's degree of action is much higher when not forced to act. The aggression-prone individual must regularly remind himself what he is trying to accomplish, to have the situation resolved in his own best interest, and remind himself that the possibility of a positive response by others is diminished when others feel forced to react. Aggression can be controlled but, at times, it may require professional help to explore the root causes of aggression to eliminate them.

Similarly, if you're shy you must realize that you miss out on fully experiencing life and all its vibrancy. Letting other people and foreign situations control your life while you merely react to circumstances is not living. The basis of shyness often is an extreme desire for personal security and a fear of taking any risks that may jeopardize what limited security you think you have. You'll realize that your extreme concern about negative evaluation is based on the false assumption that you are the center of attention. In reality, most other people are so concerned with getting by themselves, they hardly notice anyone else. You may have assumed that if others really knew you as you really are, you'd be considered of little value. You can go through life giving a performance, but that's no way to live. You realize, though, you are a unique individual. You don't have to be an actor.

If shyness is severe, a person may need to seek professional help. Most people just need to realize how many wonderful experiences in life they are missing by clutching to the limited security non-involvement appears to sustain. If you are shy, make a commitment to want to change. There are many excellent texts that can guide your transformation. By practicing exercises and learning social skills, such as how to relate to others in various situations, how to start conversations, or how to politely interrupt someone else in the midst of a conversation, shyness will no longer be a primary habit.

A Simple Formula

Whether you are shy or overly aggressive, you can get more of what you want more often, and gain immeasurable respect with one simple practice. Self-esteem will soar once this simple formula is followed: *Stop saying negative things about yourself, and start telling yourself positive things!* That means first being aware of when you say negative things about yourself, then retract the negative statement saying, "I really don't mean that! I mean I can..." For example, catch yourself when you say, "I never do well on tests." Then say, "I really don't mean that! I mean I must give myself enough time to prepare for this exam." Over time, this new habit will lead to a growth of self-esteem, and social science research has proved this one quality, self-esteem, is absolutely necessary to be a fully functioning individual.

Self-esteem cannot be stressed enough. Your level of self-esteem determines the extent of your contribution to society. Similar to a governor on an engine that allows that engine to go only so fast, self-esteem regulates the level of your individual productivity in all aspects of life. If you don't feel capable of or worthy of holding an influential career position, for example, you will not even attempt to apply. If you do not feel worthy of a close personal relationship, you will subconsciously force others to keep distance from you.

Let's use this equation to capture the dynamics involved: Self-esteem = Self-confidence + Self-respect. These are the components of self-esteem. First, you feel you are competent to live and to take on responsibilities. You know you are capable of the activities you are required to do or desire to do (self-confidence). Second, you feel you are worthy to live. You recognize that you deserve as much as anyone to be successful in career and in personal relationships (self-respect). Every person judges himself, whether he realizes it or not, by some standard or set of values. To the extent you feel you satisfy that standard or set of values, your respect for yourself grows. The important prerequisite to healthy living is to use a realistic (rather than extreme) set of values as a yardstick by which to measure your level of progress. Don't be too hard on yourself. Recognize each improvement in your skills for what it is—progress.

When you know you are making a concentrated effort to improve, you don't dissipate time and energy doubting yourself. You are able to go on with living and can bring your full intellectual and emotional powers to bear on any problem or opportunity as it arises.

Let's review. You must have self-confidence, which you gain by thinking for yourself and constructing or accepting a permanent set of values important to you. You gain self-respect by knowing that you are living those values in your life. Through use, you gain confidence in your abilities (self-confidence), and through habit formation, you believe you are as worthy of happiness as anyone (self-respect). These result in self-esteem. In turn, this self-esteem allows you to choose lofty goals and then gives you the inner strength and the focused energy to go out and accomplish those goals. The concept is simple, but the power it generates when applied brings results beyond all proportion to the effort required to implement.

Psychology of Sanity

Here is the essence of what I call "a psychology of sanity," the central part of which is a feeling of control. Control means the ability to have some affect on life situations or life circumstances to at least some extent. When you don't feel you're totally at the mercy of others, or totally at the mercy of the elements, or even totally at the mercy of chance, you are able to have hope. Even in a seemingly hopeless situation, you can:

(1) Take control of your thoughts.

You can resolutely affirm, "I will not let my mind run on about how desperate my predicament is; I will think of possibilities and will look for the seed of something positive in this difficult situation." That is the first step—controlling your thoughts. I believe there is never a hopeless situation completely beyond our control; we can always control our thoughts.

You're familiar with the old cowboy movies on TV. Picture the stereotypical scene of a stagecoach or wagon hitched to a team of horses furiously galloping

> **TRANSFORMATION:**
>
> *Stop saying negative things about yourself and start saying positive things.*
>
> "If the ear should say, 'Because I am not an eye, I do not belong to the body,' it would not for that reason cease to be part of the body. If the whole body were an eye, where would the sense of hearing be?" (1 Corinthians 12:16,17)

out of control without a driver, across the horizon. This is also a picture of the way some people react to intimidating situations. A person reacting this way lets his imagination gallop out of control, churning out a steady stream of negative thoughts. He acts as if he is the little old lady who is in the stagecoach, paralyzed with fright, and unable to take any action. There is no reason you must ever let your thoughts run out of control when, with practice, you can tell yourself, "I'm going to stop thinking about these negatives and start thinking about the possibilities available to me."

(2) After resolving to control your thoughts, survey the predicament to decide which initial steps can be taken until the next step becomes apparent.

As a walker and runner, I am familiar with what I call the *uphill phenomenon.* I'm sure you've experienced this, too. When walking uphill (especially in a steep grade and in a new environment), you were not sure how high the hill was or what was on the other side. The terrain may have been difficult. A steep grade may have forced you to slow down your pace or even to stop and rest along the way. You wondered, "How much longer must I keep going up?" As you got higher up the hill, you were able to see progressively more of what to expect, how much farther it was, and what was on the other side. You started walking, not knowing what to expect, but at least you started. You acted, and it became apparent your course of direction was correct, and in time, you knew which adjustments to make. The same is true in life. Knowing you have some control, then exercising whatever control you do have, eliminates any hopeless situations and permits you to keep sane in adversity. Begin by at least taking steps in any direction, then adjusting as you go along.

Ben's Way

Ben Franklin perfected a technique for personality training that may be of help to you. He started with a personal analysis of his own life and established which qualities or abilities were most valuable to him. For example, in his autobiography Franklin listed thirteen personality traits he considered especially valuable.

He then set out to work on these systematically, spending one week highlighting one of these traits and working to establish it as a habit. He'd write each trait down on a piece of paper and prominently display it as he worked on the trait. Once he had systematically worked on all thirteen, one at a time, he then started over with the first one on the list. He claimed for many years to have followed this regimen.

This technique has proven useful to countless individuals over the years. The first step is to establish for yourself the values you feel are most important for you to live by. Some have started with Franklin's personality traits listed below. Some have used the principles of the Bible, such as the fruits of God's Spirit enumerated in Galatians 5:22, which are love, joy, peace, patience, kindness, goodness, faithfulness, gentleness, and self-control.

Once we have established our personal values and have resolved to work on them systematically, our self-esteem begins to soar! Even when you feel you have a long way to go to perfect those values, the very fact that you are working on them has an incredible effect on your assessment of your own personal worth. "I am at least trying, and I know, in time, I will master this," you can say.

> **TRANSFORMATION:**
>
> *Self-esteem soars once you begin your personal values list and resolve to work on perfecting those qualities regularly.*
>
> "We will in all things grow up into Him who is the Head, that is, Christ." (Ephesians 4:15)

Franklin's list:

- ♦ SILENCE (unless something is worth saying)
- ♦ ORDER (putting things in place)
- ♦ RESOLUTION (perform without fail)
- ♦ FRUGALITY (waste not)
- ♦ INDUSTRY (lose no time)

- ◆ SINCERITY

- ◆ JUSTICE

- ◆ MODERATION (avoid extremes)

- ◆ CLEANLINESS

- ◆ TRANQUILITY (not disturbed by trifles)

- ◆ CHASTITY (not injuring the peace of self or others)

- ◆ HUMILITY (imitate Jesus and Socrates)

Activity

- ◆ Decide which specific time period for study and enrichment you will observe on a daily basis (even fifteen minutes, but preferably thirty minutes or more).

- ◆ Then decide which skills need to be improved specifically in your life, and list them.

- ◆ Begin working on these needed skills. Start by choosing one and begin by gathering reading material on the topic and then meditate on how to incorporate it in daily life.

- ◆ Determine to observe this regimen as a continual process for life.

Your Skills

In addition to living by values and perfecting psychological and coping skills, a successful person needs to learn more than just the rudiments of social skills. Social skills help put others at ease and help the skilled person feel in control of situations. When you're in a new environment or in an unusual situation, the adept use of social skills allows you to feel at ease and promotes cordiality in any gathering.

Education is not just increasing intellectual ability but improving in other faculties as well. You can, and I mean can, improve your natural ability, your personality, and your social skills. Your faculties are not formed and then remain stagnant once you become an adult. These faculties can and must be continually perfected as tools for successful living.

You can create your own life. You can choose to make your life interesting, exciting, and a real adventure. The successful person affirms that the quality of his life is not dependent on the environment or others. No matter how limiting circumstances may be, you still have choices. By learning and honing your skills, you're prepared to accept the exciting opportunities life is constantly introducing to you. Rather than be neutralized by fear, you have learned to neutralize the forces that cause fear by analyzing them and recognizing that when picked apart, many of these fears are mental illusions caused by negative past experiences.

> **TRANSFORMATION:**
>
> *Make it a lifelong process to daily perfect your skills in living.*

You, the successful person, have a real love for all aspects of life, the delightful and the not so delightful, since together they form the elements that make for excitement and exhilaration. By insisting on continually educating yourself (your knowledge, your abilities, and your living skills) you will be prepared to take advantage of life's interesting adventures as they come along.

"The soul takes nothing with her to the other world but her education and culture; and these, it is said, are of the greatest service or greatest injury to the dead man, at the very beginning of his journey thither." (Plato)

"Does not wisdom call out? Blessed is the man who listens to me, watching daily at my doors, waiting at my doorway. For whoever finds me finds life and receives favor from the Lord." (Proverbs 8:1,34,35)

CHAPTER 11

Dominant Dreams (Fame)

In the sixties, like most people, I was caught up in the spirit of change. Many were questioning long-held values and mores of society. I remember how passionately I felt major changes in society were needed. Much of what had been accepted for generations needed to be scrutinized since institutions that had been blindly followed no longer had the undisputed power they once had. I was swept up in this movement in the sense that I did my part to encourage others to stop and question how they could unequivocally accept governmental authority. An example of this is when those in power vacillate on public policy. Why accept blindly the edicts of some religious institution just because they claim it's the only way? Or why blindly offer your loyalty to any business conglomerate for life when it cannot grant you a job perpetually? I passionately proclaimed the message to question beliefs. This was my avocation. I didn't consider these activities work; they were what I lived for.

In time, my iconoclastic ventures gave way to more positive endeavors. Since then, I have encouraged others to question their personal habits and assumptions about life. My passion has been to identify the generalized principles of living. My avocation has been to continually research, clarify, and employ these principles of living first in my own life and then to assist others. This book is a product of my avocation.

I know others who have passions as intense as mine but in different areas. Some have a passion for gardening; for others it's nurturing a growing business. Helping others through charitable activities, embracing a discipline, such as American history, coaching winning sports teams, or even raising cattle are activities that inspire others. They have avocations, missions to which they have a commitment. The time spent is not just a job, it's bliss—a reason for living.

Our Calling

A major practical theme in scripture is the idea of a *calling*. Christians have what is referred to as a *common upward calling*, an ever-present desire and motivation to eventually attain to a level of spiritual existence to be worthy of dwelling in the presence of God. But the Bible also speaks of one's calling while on earth. Realizing that we are all born with certain abilities and propensities that would allow us to excel in some pursuit, finding one's calling or natural abilities, and pursuing a course of excellence in those areas are keys to personal fulfillment. A Christian might look at the fact that he was born with certain abilities as an indication that God wants him to develop and use those talents to God's glory.

In Matthew 25:14-30, Jesus teaches the parable of the *talents*. A master entrusted his various servants with money (talents) to invest. The servants who used those talents to enhance their master's position were commended, but the one who allowed his talents to lie dormant was punished for his slothfulness. Jesus finished the parable by saying, "For everyone who has will be given more, and he will have an abundance. Whoever does not have, even what he has will be taken from him." And in another place He said, "From the one who has been entrusted with much, much more will be asked." (Luke 12:48), as if to say to the extent we have God-given talents, our happiness and society's benefits will only be realized as we utilize and perfect those talents.

Whether you are a Christian or not, this is a powerful reason to use your abilities even if you don't feel they are God-given. Only to the extent you display and sharpen those abilities will the world benefit from your existence. The profound influence an avocation can have on one's well-being has not been stressed enough in self-development literature.

You have unfilled dreams within you waiting to become manifest; you have special dreams needing to be transformed into reality. Some of these faint visions within may have already become burning desires that are your current preoccupation, or they may still lie dormant within. You have the desire, the need, to accomplish something special with your life. In every aspect of your life, there are such motivational goals. We've discussed some of these. You have a need to succeed in your career, your personal life (including friends and family), and a mission to connect with the universe (God), but there is still a special need that must be addressed. I suggest there are unique dreams that have to do with inherent abilities and talents that must not be neglected but must be allowed to thrive. Identify and pursue these.

Providence has endowed each of us with special talents and abilities. Science has shown that within our genetic makeup are the seeds of special gifts, whether they be physical or mental attributes. In time, these kernels of talent or ability will naturally begin to take root and grow as long as they are not deliberately stifled. This is a natural inclination, just as natural as the inclination of a seed to sprout once placed in soil. We will always feel something is missing unless we allow these natural forces to incubate within us and grow to fruition. Though we may not be able to claim total responsibility for putting these talents there in the first place, we do have the responsibility to provide the environment that allows the seed-talents and potential to germinate (by desire and dream) and then to grow to reality, becoming manifest to and benefiting others.

You will never be satisfied until you use these special gifts. What good is a profound musical talent if not used? What good is exceptional mathematical ability if not exercised? We sense these talents are wasted if they're not used. Discover, uncover, and display these hidden talents. I'll offer ways in which you can utilize your personal gifts daily. Think what additional enjoyment this will bring! Admit your profound mission to use your talents commensurate with your potential, pursuing your own special dreams.

Abraham Maslow, one of the fathers of self-improvement psychology, spoke of this need as "self-actualization." This is the human condition of striving for and reaching our potential in some aspects of our lives. Our self-satisfaction and self-esteem soars when we feel our talents are not lying dormant but are being exercised. We experience self-actualization when we feel that we are displaying our individuality. We are producing evidence that we can point to—proving we are unique; we have talents others do not have; we have left a mark during our time in this world. We feel we have become or are becoming what we are intended to be. Our unique talents have not been squandered.

I remember the feeling that came over me as I held each of my children when they were newly born. They were bursting with the freshness of life and all sorts of possibilities. And as a father, I know I hoped desperately that they'd blossom and become the persons they were meant to be with all their innate talents and gifts being used to the full. I'm sure every parent feels the same. In fact, many concerned parents watch their children carefully, and when they see a talent emerging, they encourage it immediately. They spend money to provide their children with classes or instruction in the emerging talent whether it be music, dance, or some other ability. They tend and cultivate their children so they'll bloom. Yet, as adults, some people stop setting aside time to pursue their own special gifts. What a tragedy!

The distribution of talents in the world should be of little concern to us. Some may have talents that are in high demand and may produce immediate benefits in terms of financial remuneration. Some actors, entertainers, entrepreneurs, and athletes are fortunate to be granted financial success by using their extraordinary abilities. To others, their talents may not be of immediate financial reward; nonetheless, their talents are valuable. Some may be blessed to have had a far-reaching effect on society, gaining notoriety through an invention or discovery. Others may only affect a small circle of friends or associates. Nevertheless, a similar satisfaction is shared—each makes a contribution. The point is not what talents we have, but that we use these talents!

Have you had the satisfaction yet of seeing your own talents bud and then flower to be enjoyed by others? Have you ever thought of this? Whenever you use your talents, you are simultaneously and invariably experiencing enjoyment. Consequently, the more you use your talents, the more your life pleasure increases. As you maximize your talent effectiveness and strive for your potential, your enjoyment and satisfaction also increase.

I'm sure you've seen films of wild birds who have been nurtured back to health while in captivity after an accident. While regaining their strength they are caged and immobilized. The moment they are let loose and flap their wings, though they haven't flown for months, they fly unassisted. That moment may be as much of an exhilaration to an observer as to the birds. You can't help but sense the ecstasy of the moment as they soar and glide completely free and unrestricted. As they soar, you sense the complete, unbounded pleasure and feeling of power that such birds experience because they are able to use their abilities in the way they were intended. You have the opportunity to experience the same sensation when you fully use your innate talents.

Avocation

Within each person is a desire to make a difference, to make a mark, to feel somehow his stay here has not been in vain. It's our dream. It's our avocation. By avocation, I mean a personal calling or mission in life. Whether we feel a driving need to excel in some area, or simply to build self-esteem, or demonstrate excellence in some facet of our lives is a need. I use the word *fame* to remind myself of this need to be different, unique, or noted in some talent or ability. Many are able to fulfill this need through their careers or occupations, but this may not always be possible. To some, an avocation may mean a career; to others, it may mean a hobby. In all cases, an avocation provides an opportunity to excel in some talent or ability, to engage in a project that is intensely interesting and exciting, to have a creative outlet, and to experience growth and build self-esteem.

I know of major corporate executives whose real fascination is tinkering with motors and engines. This avocation provides an outlet for their creative mechanical abilities. They look forward to the change of pace a hobby provides along with yet another opportunity to display different talents of which they are proud. Perhaps they feel they have gone as far as they wish in their careers and appreciate having another avenue of creative expression. I know of others who have occupations that don't allow them to use their abilities to the fullest. For them, an avocation provides such an outlet. What is more, their careers may not provide the desired opportunity for advancement or even fame. An avocation offers the chance to stand out. For instance, 20 percent of the employee population is involved in some aspect of manufacturing plant operations. The manufacturing job may not require any specialized knowledge or provide outlets for creativity. However, an interesting hobby can offer this in abundance. I have friends who feel like just another cog in the corporate wheel, but their involvement in local politics allows them the opportunity to be heard and to make a difference in their own environments.

> **TRANSFORMATION:**
>
> *Don't be concerned with the distribution of talents; be concerned with finding, using, and, most of all, enjoying your talents.*
>
> "We have different gifts, according to the grace given us." (Romans 12:6)

Activity

ASK THESE QUESTIONS:

If you are looking for an activity that you can really enjoy or for a career that brings excitement, ponder for a moment the tasks you enjoy doing. Career counselors frequently ask their clients to answer these questions:

◆ If I had a million dollars in the bank and did not have to work, what would I like to do?

◆ If money were no object, which activities would give me the opportunity to keep growing in ability?

◆ Which activities did I really enjoy when I was younger, even as a child or an adolescent?

◆ Which activities have I given up, for one reason or another, that I look back on with fondness and a desire to take up again?

◆ Which areas of interest still hold a fascination for me, and which topics would I really like to explore in far greater detail?

Answers to any of these questions will provide clues to your undeveloped abilities and desires. These ideas, once identified, will give direction in career and/or avocation choice.

Spend a little time considering your answers to the previous questions to isolate the talents, hobbies, or abilities you have. Pick at least one of them and resolve to use the suggestions throughout the rest of this chapter to perfect your talent or hobby.

Your ultimate goal will be to eventually merge vocation and avocation into one, if possible. However, this may not always be possible. For instance, some may have retired from a career and may use a newly found avocation as an avenue for continued growth and validation of self-esteem. Others may be in a high-paying occupation and realize that it would be an economic hardship to go from a top career salary to, at best, a minimal salary as a trainee in another field. The economic realities inhibit some from reaching for their true work-related passions. However, this hesitance to leave seeming security or to abandon responsibilities as a parent and family provider need not stifle opportunities for growth.

A starting point for career renewal or for additional growth in tandem with present career is an avocation. Your growth and quest for meaningful activities need never be put on hold. Your dream to make a difference in society or to distinguish yourself in some field can always be pursued, if not full-time, then at least part-time.

The Possibilities

Your ultimate goal is to merge vocation and avocation. One option may be leaving employment at one firm and moving to another that will allow you to use the talents you possess. However, if this option is one you seriously consider, *wait*. The first step is to explore the possibilities in your current position. You may be able to shift your priorities in your present position. Your present job description may include a number of duties, some of which you enjoy and that challenge your talents, while some may not. Is it possible to enter into an agreement with your department head or superior to have your job description focused more specifically on the tasks that stimulate your talents? Help your supervisor see that maximizing time spent on tasks you do well is in the best interests of the organization, too. To spend your time in the area where you excel will increase productivity inside the organization. Your position may, for example, include a sales function and a customer service function. Your forte may be in sales. To focus strictly on the function that you enjoy and do well (sales) and then to transfer the responsibility for after-sales follow-up to another person who is better suited for that function, is to maximize the talents of all those involved. The organization reaps the benefits in terms of increased sales and more accommodating customer service. Concentrating on what you enjoy and eliminating tasks you find tedious motivate you to excel.

Another option is to ask to be transferred to a department within your firm that could best utilize your abilities. I know of someone in an advertising agency who realized he really enjoyed discovering trends in society. To him it was as satisfying as solving a mystery to be among the first to isolate and identify an emerging attitude shift in public perception. He asked to be transferred from the marketing department that dealt with the practical applications of working with specific clients, to the research department that dealt with more abstract issues and trends. He found his new assignment of designing and conducting national

> **TRANSFORMATION:**
>
> *Work toward incorporating your avocation with your vocation with the ultimate goal of merging the two.*
>
> "For where your treasure is there your heart will be also."
> (Luke 12:34)

surveys to be extremely exciting. Devising specific questions that could more accurately ferret out respondents' attitudes was very challenging to him. Going to work was no longer a drudgery but an adventure. This transformation was made possible because he was determined to find the work he enjoyed, and he persisted in requesting a transfer.

A third option, also within your present firm, may be to volunteer for an assignment as it comes up, one that will challenge your abilities. I met someone in a large organization who dreamed of one day becoming a writer. She resigned herself to the fact that since she had no experience in writing, her chances of being accepted for a position as a columnist or editor were very slim. Besides, for her to accept a pay cut to take a job she might better enjoy would require a great sacrifice for her family, a sacrifice she felt she could not conscientiously ask them to make. However, when her organization considered instituting a company newsletter for its employees, she volunteered for the assignment. She would continue her present responsibilities but would take on this additional responsibility. The department manager was delighted to find someone who willingly accepted this project.

At first, the assignment meant extra work and the juggling of her work load. However, since she enjoyed writing and had a definite ability, the assignment was a joy. She gained immense satisfaction. Due to her talent, the newsletter was an immediate success and was expanded. She was named editor of the newsletter, and some of her former responsibilities were passed to others in the office. Though this assignment as newsletter editor was not a full-time position, and she was required to continue some relatively dull tasks, she is now able to spend an appreciable amount of time doing what she considers inspiring and enjoyable. At the same time, she did not have to ask her family to suffer a diminished lifestyle while she pursued a new career path. Her position now allows her to write stories about various employees and publish anecdotes that emphasize the corporate culture. Her newsletter has become an asset to the organization. This happened because she isolated the abilities she felt she'd like to perfect and expand in her life and then looked for an opportunity to cultivate her talents. She has been able to effectively merge her vocation with her avocation. Her career is much more interesting, and her fellow employees have also benefited.

For some, this transformation has required leaving one company and going to work for another that would allow for a wider variety of responsibilities. Many have realized that staying with their former employer would never allow them the opportunity to utilize their talents. They have sought new jobs that entail responsibilities that now challenge their abilities and incorporate their talents. For some, this has required merely going to a different corporation in the same industry, a corporation that did have an opening and that considered their experience in the field an asset while allowing them to broaden their duties.

For others, the quest for a merging of avocation and vocation has required looking for a new position in a new industry. Sometimes additional training or schooling is required. I know of many who have met the challenge by going to school in the evenings while continuing to support themselves and/or families during the day in a job that was dull and repetitive. The dream of a new career motivated them to persevere. They kept the goal in sight, and the time required, though perhaps four or five years, was worth the sacrifice since they now enjoy a career that employs their talents and inherent abilities. They eventually merged their vocations and avocations.

Striking Out, Not Striking Out

For still others, the only possible solution is to strike out on their own, starting their own businesses. Someone with an entrepreneurial spirit will never be satisfied working for someone else who will not allow them free reign of the creative process. To the vast majority of entrepreneurs, the incentive to start new businesses is not the dream of financial fortune so much as the dream of being able to use their talents to produce products or services of which they can be proud. They crave the opportunity to pursue careers they can enjoy. Since they are good at what they enjoy, they usually become very successful. Financial rewards have accrued because they first were tenacious enough and brave enough to follow their dreams and daring enough to try something that would better utilize their talents. For them the only way to quiet their restive spirits was to attempt to bring their idea to reality. Other jobs they had had were too structured to allow them the latitude to experiment and innovate. Entrepreneurship permitted the flow of ideas that satisfied their need for creativity. They have merged their avocation and vocation by first creating a company that would provide the career opportunities best suited to them.

I know someone who did exactly that. Jerry was an underwriter for an insurance company. Well-schooled in insurance coverage and law, he sat behind a desk rating and issuing insurance policies. He felt restricted and limited in the use of his talents. He wanted to be with people and to feel he was helping them. He was in touch with his interests enough to know he would not really enjoy sales work, but he was confident that when the right opportunity appeared he would know it. Shortly after making the decision to begin looking, he was offered a consulting position with a large manufacturer that wanted independent advice and someone to oversee their insurance program. Jerry jumped at the chance. He resigned his position and offered his services as a risk management consultant, first to one company, and then by referral to others. As a risk manager, he helps his clients design loss control and insurance programs. He shows them how to limit the cost of insurance by using techniques such as self-funding and safety planning. Daily he works directly with corporate personnel, custom-tailoring programs that help them protect their assets and feel secure while minimizing costs. In this position he uses his analytical ability to consider all possible eventualities systematically and to logically predict how to minimize the risks of each. Jerry has bragged to me on numerous occasions, "I haven't had to work a day in my life since I started my consulting firm. What I do is not work—it's fun!"

> **TRANSFORMATION:**
>
> *Progressively work to perfect your abilities and talents to benefit both yourself and society.*
>
> "If the whole body were an eye, where would the sense of hearing be? If they were all one part, where would the body be?" (1 Corinthians 12:17,19)

What About a Hobby?

For you, this craving for creative reign and need to perfect your talents may be satisfied by pursuing a hobby after business hours. Many have told me that they enjoy their jobs and enjoy the friends with whom they work. They would never want to give up the friendships and security that their present jobs provide. Still, they have that need to be creative. A hobby provides that outlet. Many people enjoy playing with their home computers. This hobby enables them to further their education, perfect talents different from the ones they use in their occupations, while providing an avenue for creativity.

One of the most contented men I've known didn't have a college education. In fact, he never finished high school, but he had gained wisdom from life experiences. Due to his limited education, his work choices were also limited. He wasn't able to find an occupation that was also an avocation, so he labored as a carpenter, and later as a machinist. This manual labor suited him well; he could see the end product of his efforts. An assembly line job didn't motivate him. He took pride in his work and saw the fruits of his labor. He could have developed his abilities to become a craftsman. However, he recognized he didn't have the necessary entrepreneurial spirit. He was content to do the next best thing and excel in his vocation to provide for his family. He had what he wanted, and he maintained good health due to his physical exercise on the job.

He got most of his satisfaction and contentment from his avocation, though. The focal point of his day's efforts was always directed toward his charitable activities. Working through his church, he maintained a busy schedule of activities to help others. Religiously (and this term applies in several ways here), he devoted at least fifteen hours a week to a variety of activities that included study, church functions, visitations, and other charitable efforts. Although his avocation never integrated into a career, it gave him the daily opportunity to feel useful, to do something that mattered, and to engage in a meaningful activity. His avocation provided purpose for his life and gave him something of which he could be proud. It allowed him to give something back to others and extend far beyond himself. For some forty years he continued without any observable limit to his motivation. I know this because he was my father. The quiet contentment and satisfaction he exuded live on as an example and fond memory in the lives of those his efforts touched.

Review

Let's look at some of the options available to you. Your priority will be to see your vocation and avocation converge into one. Your wish may be to spend 100 percent of your time working at that which you really enjoy. Perhaps, though, you may be content to spend a portion of your day working on projects that you feel fulfill your calling or mission in life. The possibilities to do this are:

- ◆ To be an entrepreneur and found your own company

- ◆ To arrange your present job description to include predominantly responsibilities that make use of your talents

- ◆ To transfer to a different department within the same firm that allows for more freedom in pursuing your passion

- ◆ To find an opportunity outside of your present career or company that will permit fulfillment of your abilities

- ◆ To arrange your job description to include at least some time for activities aligned with your calling

- ◆ To use your hobby as a means to cultivate your abilities

With all these possibilities there are no excuses for not being able to pursue activities that are your passion. Even if you find commitments presently do not allow you to spend the majority of your time on your personal priorities, at least some time each day can be devoted to pursuing your bliss. Some people spend two hours each evening after their work day devoted to fulfilling their potential. This time, along with five hours on each weekend day, yields a total of twenty hours a week, or one thousand a year, doing what they love.

Imagine a thousand hours per year devoted to projects about which you feel passionate, projects that can make a difference to your immediate world, projects that are fulfilling your potential!

We human beings have an innate desire to feel good about ourselves, to feel we are special, worthy of respect. The perfecting of our talents and abilities is one basis for self-esteem. I hope you have chosen or will choose a career that allows you to do just that—perfect your talents. However, if you have not been able to do this fully due to circumstances, your avocation or hobby gives you the opportunity. By spending time in an area you personally enjoy, growth comes naturally and with little effort. As you grow in expertise, your self-esteem also grows. Choosing a field of interest and one about which you feel enthusiastic gives you the impetus to continue learning and continue perfecting your skills without self-imposed limitations.

Having an avocation permits you to become an absolute expert and authority in some field of endeavor providing you with all the more reason for feeling good about yourself. This should not be necessary. Recognizing we are part of God's family should be enough of a basis for self-esteem, but in reality most of us seem to want something we can point to as a basis for feeling special. An avocation or hobby serves that need.

Ultimately, our endeavors should lead to a level of activity that psychologist Abraham Maslow called *self-actualization*, the state of becoming all that you are capable of. If you have chosen a field of interest about which you feel passionate, you are already motivated to grow. You naturally want to be all you are capable of becoming.

Any figure skater, when asked why she spends the grueling hours in training, will say she does it because she loves the sport; it's simply enjoyment. That may appear to be a selfish reply. However, think of all the thousands of spectators at the skaters' exhibitions who are mesmerized and who marvel at the skaters' abilities. What at first appears selfish provides a benefit to many. Any productive avocation one pursues, even for selfish enjoyment, benefits humanity.

Self-actualization involves losing our *self* in a project or endeavor to the point where we labor not so much for self-interest but out of the desire for fulfillment. Our efforts are focused more on the desire to give back to others, to bring pleasure to others, to ferret out knowledge for the sake of helping others. Chapter 5 on "Spirituality" detailed this inherent need within us to find our place in the universe or to recognize our connection with all around us. An avocation provides us with an opportunity to give back to society. Our efforts can provide stimulation, pleasure, and advancement for others. We feel contented that we have, in our own way, been able to contribute to society.

TRANSFORMATION:

Consider your avocation as the pursuit of higher order needs (self-actualization).

"We have different gifts, according to the grace given us. If it is contributing to the needs of others, let him give generously; if it is leadership, let him govern diligently; if it is showing mercy, let him do it cheerfully." (Romans 12:6,8)

Since we are doing something we passionately enjoy, this process is a natural progression. We don't need to force ourselves to give unselfishly; it comes automatically. An avocation, then, nurtures our self-esteem needs, our need for self-actualization, and our spiritual needs.

Many leaders in industry who have garnered all the possible accolades in their field, have said, "I just had a need to give back to the industry that has been so good to me." I have found it interesting that they frequently use the exact same words to describe their desire: "I just had to give back," "I just felt the need to do something for others."

Your avocation or calling, incorporated in your vocation, makes it easier to arrive at this point in life. However, the pursuit of any avocation (independent, if necessary, from a career vocation) will eventually lead you to the enviable position of having both the credentials and the desire to look beyond yourself and really feel you are benefiting others.

You will, by arranging your time, sense your life is vital. Your life is an adventure. Each day is filled with activities that delight you. You look forward to each day with the knowledge that you will be able to engage in at least one project that will further your fulfillment in life, a project that will daily justify your existence to yourself.

I previously asked the question, "What would life be like if you could love your work?" I conclude this chapter by asking, "What would your life be like if you daily pursued your passion?"

"If one advances confidently in the direction of his dreams, and endeavors to live the life which he has imagined, he will meet with a success unexpected in common hours." (Henry David Thoreau)

"What the righteous desire will be granted." (Proverbs 10:24)

CHAPTER 12

The Secret of Balance

I've developed a habit that has been very valuable to me. This habit has kept life interesting and exciting for me. This is how it works. I regularly ask myself, "Am I satisfied with how my life is going now?" At one point when I asked this question I didn't feel the overwhelming sense of security I once had. "But why?" I wondered. After considering the eight facets of my life one at a time, I traced the discomfort to my business. I realized the business was not performing as efficiently or growing at the rate it had in the past. I had been spending more time on my hobbies and not devoting enough time to day-to-day operations of the business. I had lost sight of the fact that my family's well-being and the well-being of fellow employees and their families was being jeopardized. I immediately re-prioritized and strategized till I felt comfortable with my recommitment to business. While planning, I identified several new projects that rekindled my enthusiasm for business growth. What I did was make a decision to rebalance my priorities to fit current changing circumstances. Time and again I have used this self-monitoring mechanism to insure that no aspect of life would get out of control.

Many of us feel our lives are constant juggling acts. We are torn in many directions. At times we may feel stressed by pressures as they pile up. Life is a struggle, and we may find it difficult to control our mental and emotional equilibrium. Whenever we experience such severe strain on time and capacity, the enjoyment for living dissipates. Balance is a simple principle which will release pressure and bring back enjoyment.

The Scriptures are filled with individuals who, to their own detriment, were extreme in their pursuit of various causes. We are told of Ananias and Sapphira who were extreme in the love of money. The Apostle Peter said, "You have not lied to men but to God." (Acts 5:4) Jesus in the Sermon on the Mount asked us to consider, "Who of you by worrying can add a single hour to his life? Since you cannot do this very little thing, why do you worry about the rest?" (Luke 12:25) The emphasis has always been on balance, on refraining extremes. The Scriptures direct us, "So whether you eat or drink or whatever you do, do it all for the glory of God." (1 Corinthians 10:31) Sometimes we ignore two simple principles: *limitations* and *change*.

With so many possibilities open to us, there are limits as to what we can do even though the choices are unlimited. It may be difficult to live among potentially unlimited possibilities and yet be forced to limit (to choose) our own possibilities. If we are to live without constantly juggling the various aspects of life and not doing a particularly good job at any, we must accept limitations. We have to make choices in pursuits and choices in time allocation.

What makes limits more acceptable is the understanding that our choices can and do change over time. Though we limit our time in certain endeavors, we are perfectly capable of changing our priorities and our pursuits over time. If we understand these two principles—limits and change—and live by them, life does not have to be a "struggle to juggle." Regardless of what we choose, living requires a balancing act. However, that balancing act can seem overwhelming if we feel we're juggling four balls at once. Or we can look at the balancing act more like the balance required to ride a bicycle. The former activity is difficult to maintain and can be very strenuous (juggling), while the latter (bicycling) is a balance that becomes second nature. It need not be strenuous and can be maintained virtually without effort. You have the opportunity to structure your chosen responsibilities in either of the two ways. Both require the act of balancing, but balancing need not be laborious. You make the choice!

Life Course Model

One thing that makes the acceptance of limitations more palatable is the concept of the *Adult Life Course Model*. This viewpoint proposes that adults shape their lives, or allow their lives to be shaped, but at predictable intervals will step back and evaluate where they are and what they have done, and make necessary changes. This proposition suggests there is a common sequence during the course of the adult life that allows for first the structuring of our lives followed by a period of self-examination. The concept was proposed by Daniel Levinson and popularized by Gail Sheehy, who described the process in her book, *Passages.* The point is, our opportunities change as we grow in understanding and experience. Once exposed to self-examination, we may choose to discontinue one activity and replace it with another. At predictable times in life, around age twenty-one, age thirty, and again at mid-life we are faced with the need to make assessments about where our lives are going. If we don't deal with life at these critical points, we risk perpetual emptiness.

Though it may be an oversimplification, this model proposes that the developmental stages through which an adult proceeds will usually follow a predictable pattern though the choices made will be individual and personal. As adults age and experience life, their outlooks change. The adult may not consciously detect a change in viewpoint and may proceed through a life developmental stage without realizing that transition has occurred. If an adult succeeds in completing the work of growth required during each stage, the transition to the next is not difficult. However, if an adult (due to environmental pressure, mental or emotional immaturity) does not fully integrate development into his life at a preceding stage, then succeeding stages will become progressively more difficult to negotiate.

You will face choices at each transition stage. Between the ages of eighteen and twenty-one, an individual will accept certain socially expected roles of adult life, such as recognizing his or her own autonomy as a person. During this period as an adult, one is expected to declare independence from parents and make choices regarding education, career, eventual marriage, and future family status.

Somewhere between the ages of twenty-eight and thirty-two one can expect to go through a transition assessing what has been accomplished up to this point in adult life. One could note some of the things that have been missed or put off. If one believes he has been herded by society into a certain role, he may make radical directional changes in life. Life goals are reaffirmed or altered during this stage. This transition is generally followed by a period where one finds a *place in society*. We speak of adults *settling down*. We may immerse ourselves in family and/or career. This period occupies one's time through the thirties.

The late thirties, or perhaps as late as age forty-five, one can expect to go through another transition period. Chronologically, it is a mid-life transition, and during this time, adults become extremely aware that life is at least half over. They acknowledge either consciously or in action that they are mortal and often feel they have one more chance to restructure their lives. This may entail major modifications. Some people repudiate their past values and actions, while others reaffirm and feel a stronger commitment to their values.

As adults progress through their fifties and sixties, they begin to accept and later fully understand their limitations and mortality. During this period, adults frequently realize that they have an opportunity to give back to society, using their abilities while accepting their weaknesses. When adults reach an age over sixty-five, society begins to think of them as old. However, though in this interval they must come to terms with their limiting physical capabilities, they can continue to grow mentally, emotionally, and spiritually.

The value of employing this adult life course model is that it highlights the fact that we are continually changing and are confronted with choices. Acknowledging that we go through developmental transitions will allow us to navigate them consciously rather than be forced by circumstances to just accept change. We can choose rather than have choices made for us. We choose the values, the goals, and the extent to which we will pursue those goals in each of the eight areas of life previously mentioned. We can decide, then reaffirm or alter our commitments. The pressures that some experience while attempting to juggle responsibilities in the eight life spheres are due to not consciously making choices but accepting choices made for them by others or by circumstances. Balance is possible by recognizing we are in the driver's seat and deciding where we wish to go.

Realizing we can make choices to maintain or regain our balance makes the journey less threatening and more adventurous. The fabled *mid-life crisis* need not be a crisis at all, but actually a reaffirmation of joys still ahead.

If we have not satisfactorily resolved various issues in our lives previously, early adulthood or mid-life may be the time when these neglected or suppressed areas begin to nag at us. Being forewarned, we can decide to what extent we will confront this gap and regain balance. A woman who may have given all to the nurturing of her family earlier in life must decide the extent to which she will use the time now to establish or reestablish a career or avocation. A career executive who has become an established success must decide whether he will make significant changes in his relationships with family and friends if they were not previously given priority time.

Knowing Yourself

As you go through life transitions, you may not realize why you feel unhappy, restless, or depressed. Something is missing, but what? If you are attuned to yourself, though, you will realize these feelings are an indication you need to regain balance in your life. You can recognize the twinge of longing or regret and stop suppressing a craving for fulfillment in a particular life area. This requires listening to your agitated subconscious, but it's not difficult. Make a conscious affirmation that you are seeking that which is missing. That affirmation will immediately begin a process. Over time, thoughts and ideas will begin to surface, leading you toward what you've neglected. You can do this whenever you feel any dull sensation that something is missing, but don't wait for an apparent crisis.

Review the eight areas of life, B-A-L-A-N-C-E-D:

♦ Body (fitness)

♦ Allegiance (faith)

- ◆ Legacy (family)

- ◆ Affluence (fortune)

- ◆ Networks (friends)

- ◆ Career (finances)

- ◆ Education (faculties)

- ◆ Dreams (fame)

Ask, "Am I experiencing satisfaction in each life facet? What more must I do if I am to feel a sense of peace?"

Asking these questions at transition points may lead you to distinguish a difference between your vocation and your avocation. You may sense that while you have met with career success, there are other quests worth pursuing. Whatever the conflict turns out to be, the next step is the same. Allow your inner voice the opportunity to suggest possible ways of resolving the conflict. Pray for guidance and be open to the leadings.

For instance, mid-life may be the first time you are forced to confront the physical dimension of life. You may have taken your health for granted, and only when the inevitable aches and pains are encountered are you reminded of what you have neglected. You are being led to renew a commitment to that which you neglected. Don't become obsessed with any one life aspect to the detriment of others. For instance, becoming obsessed with body age, mourning the loss of some vitality when there are many rich experiences still ahead, would be a mistake. Dwelling on the negative and forgetting the positive is always a major

> **TRANSFORMATION:**
>
> *All of us can expect to go through predictable periods of transition, times when we reorder our lives.*
>
> "Be transformed by the renewing of your mind. Then you will be able to test and approve what God's will is—His good, pleasing and perfect will."
> (Romans 12:2)

error. It's true—mid-life may mean some loss of vitality, but it also brings with it a period of more leisure time. (Usually one's career is established, and children are more able to fend for themselves.) This may be the time to renew the link to posterity and society through volunteer work, service work, or other activities to give to others.

Again, use the B-A-L-A-N-C-E-D checklist. The list will help you readily call to mind the major life areas. Just ask, "Is any one of the B-A-L-A-N-C-E-D aspects of life being forgotten?"

Be aware that your values may change over time, or at least the order of their importance may need rearranging. What you desire and what is of most importance at one point in life may be of lesser urgency at another point. Over time, you may even let go of some long-standing values because they don't hold meaning for you now. You may be startled to realize that some values you accepted earlier in life without critical evaluation. Once life experience (perhaps a particular incident) forces you to grapple with your priorities, you come to a clearer picture of what you value.

Julie had such an experience. Once she progressed past her teenage years, she admitted that peer popularity was not as important as it once was. She even admitted that the desire to be popular placed undue restrictions on her life. With this revelation, Julie was no longer held captive by self-imposed limitations. This meant personal growth. Without regular review and prioritizing of values, she may never have detected the extent of the influence. Because she paid attention when she felt out of balance, she recognized that her self-deprecation and lack of ambition and were symptoms of the need to reassess values and a need to advance.

A Time For Re-evaluation

Regularly perform the values exercise previously suggested. Schedule time to meditate first upon the values that motivate you, then prioritize these values, putting them in order of importance. Ask yourself whether you are living in harmony with the values you have chosen.

When I conduct seminars, I give attendees the opportunity to order their priorities. I find from anonymous surveys of the attendees where values such as physical health, loving and being loved, and the importance of a close family invariably appear near the top of the list. When asked to do a personal evaluation, though, attendees frequently admit that they have not been giving much consideration to their values.

The next step after evaluation is considering the changes necessary to put your life more in harmony with your values, more in line with your needs. Here use the B-A-L-A-N-C-E-D checklist and ask one by one, "Am I neglecting any one of these areas of my life?" Once you admit to yourself that you have been neglecting a valuable life facet, it should become clear which adjustments are necessary. You may find it necessary to include time for growth in this aspect of life. This may not mean allocating more time for one pursuit but only rescheduling time so you can fit in your pursuit of this neglected goal. This is an example of fine-tuning the balance in your life to reflect changing circumstances.

Some have reported to me that they have received an unexpected feeling of exhilaration when they have simply made room for some of these values important to them. All that was needed was admitting that something was missing, detecting what it was, and rearranging schedules to include the forgotten value. Some have reported tremendous benefits after making room for such things as harmony in their relations with others, the building of a positive faith, the willingness to share their blessings with others, the striving to understand with an open mind rather than immediately objecting to the viewpoint of another, and the display of love by actions for others. The willingness to put into practice what they knew to be important was all that was missing—a simple acknowledgment and a conscious resolve: "I will work on displaying this week this aspect of character I hold to be valuable." An inspiration and a disciplined resolve provided the impetus to bring actions more into harmony with personal desires. Balance had been restored.

True Balance

Balance in life is similar to the balance you learned when learning to ride a bicycle. Bike riding requires physical balance. Riding through life requires mental and emotional balance. Now, stop and think about when you first learned to ride a bicycle. It was not difficult, and you probably learned in a matter of days, at the most a few weeks, once you decided you wanted to learn how to ride. You will find the skill of maintaining balance in life is easily acquired once you understand the concept. When learning bike-riding, you were first taught the proper position for safe riding: both hands firmly on the handle bars, properly seated, feet on the pedals and mind attentive to the terrain. Balance in life is accomplished in the same way. Life balance means having a firm hand on all eight aspects of life, being aware of all eight facets and the need for fulfillment in each, and making the effort to systematically display these facets.

As a novice bike rider, carefully holding your position took a lot of effort. In time and with practice, you were able to ride with only one hand on the handle bars; then you were able to stand up and pedal. You could take your feet off the pedals and you could perhaps even ride no-handed, and you still kept your balance! What was the secret? You first consciously and carefully practiced the basics. In time you could take more liberties but always got back to the basics. When riding carefree but coming upon rough terrain, you quickly focused on your position on the bike, didn't you? When turning a corner, especially if you were riding one- or no-handed, you quickly focused with your hands back on the handle bars. Balance, then, does not mean having to firmly posi-

> **TRANSFORMATION:**
>
> *A periodic re-evaluation of priorities is necessary.*
>
> "Seek first the kingdom and His righteousness, and all these things (material things mentioned previously) will be given to you as well." (Matthew 6:33)

tion yourself at all times; it just means recognizing the importance of each bicycle function, knowing when to make full contact with all of them and doing so regularly.

This is true in life. Once you are an experienced "rider" and have made connection with all eight aspects of your life and partially put them in order, there will be times when you give one life area more attention than others. Balance does not mean equal time and equal attention to all. Balance can be attained even when neglecting one or two areas deliberately, just as you can ride a bicycle without holding both handles, or you can coast for a while without putting your feet on either pedal. The important point with balance is making a deliberate decision: "I will of necessity, have to neglect this important aspect of life temporarily, but I will not be far away from any neglected life role for very long."

For example, during a period when you desire career growth you may realize you need further education. This may require enrolling in a community college at night while working during the day. As a result, you may not be able to spend as much time with friends or family. After serious analysis and consultation with spouse and others affected, you decide you are willing to selectively limit your attention to several life aspects (family and friends) in order to grow in another area of life. Since you have made a conscious decision and are willing to pay the price, there is no reason to berate yourself for neglecting growth in one area for growth in another.

The other critical point is that you have resolved not to neglect friends and family indefinitely. You have not put them totally out of mind. You may give them somewhat less attention, but you explain beforehand why you feel this is necessary. Being conscious that family and friends are extremely important, you resolve to give them extra attention during school breaks. During the summer, between semesters, you plan a leisurely vacation with your spouse and children, devoting extra attention to their needs at this time. Similarly with friends, you apologize for having to decline invitations but promise yourself that during summer break you will plan several barbecue parties inviting those people with whom you reluctantly had to limit association. Since you have spoken to all affected by your decision, and since you have resolved that this selective inattention will be for a limited period, you have no regrets about your decision. All eight facets of your self continue to be accounted for. Your life is still in balance.

♦ *You* have made the decision, not someone else. You have analyzed the consequences of your actions and are willing to accept the negatives of your decision.

♦ You have resolved that this selective oversight will not be for an indefinite period. You have limited the negative effects of your decision. You firmly assert that you remain aware of and account for all eight life facets.

Periodic Audits

Balanced people will periodically take stock of their current location in their life course journey. Some may have scheduled regular audits of their life. Many use the extra time off from responsibilities during holidays to fit in a substantial block of time to perform this audit. During this analysis they assess where they have been and what they will do to eliminate a total void in any one life sphere. Some find it useful to go down the B-A-L-A-N-C-E-D checklist weekly when they do their weekly planning to be certain all eight categories have been given consideration. This way none is neglected for any inordinate period.

You are astute enough to realize that when you feel your life is not complete or you have somehow lost that reassuring sense of well-being in your life, you can return to wholeness through a *balance audit*. When a period of life transition or period of exceeding pressure comes, you will firmly grasp and make solid contact with all eight roles. As a balanced life traveler, you will be like the cyclist who comes upon rocky terrain and uses the first few jarring bumps to remind himself to hold on tightly with both hands firmly grasping the handlebars, giving extra attention to his balance. When pressures arise or when a change of course is necessary (like the cyclist who is confronted with a sharp bend in the road) make contact with your eight life connections.

Your Personal Inventory

In each of your eight dimensions, you have a set of values which you consider to be desirable. You have a picture of what the epitome of family life would be for you, what your realistic ideal would be in physical health, and how important wealth and affluence are to you. It will be helpful when doing a personal inventory of the eight dimensions to have goals in each. On paper, write out specifically what each dimension means to you.

♦ What do you desire in each area?

♦ How will you attain each?

♦ In which order will you work on each life area?

♦ Which aspects of your life do you presently feel especially deficient in?

> **TRANSFORMATION:**
> *Balance does not mean equal time but does mean equal consideration to each life dimension.*

Make a solemn promise to never shortchange yourself. You will be a whole person, experiencing the best that is available to you in each facet of life. You will practice integrity by never knowingly eliminating any essential dimensions of your growth. You promise to be faithful to all your values, working on each in succession.

Recipe for Happiness

The B-A-L-A-N-C-E-D list might be considered a recipe for fulfillment in life. There are eight special ingredients to this recipe. The elimination of any one ingredient will not produce the desired repast (a fulfilled life). Conversely, remember there is no consensus on how a good food should taste. One person may prefer baked goods a little sweeter than another, but an over-abundance of sugar far out of proportion to the other ingredients will spoil the final product. Also, the elimination of this one ingredient (sugar) altogether will force you to say "something is missing here." Furthermore, you have probably found that you prefer the proportion of the ingredients modified somewhat in your favorite recipes, but for the products to taste good, you never apply excessive amounts of one ingredient or totally eliminate another. Your recipe for life fulfillment will include all eight dimensions of being. Your fulfillment, happiness, and well-being will depend on faithfulness to your values in each area of life. Similarly, you establish your own identity by working out the perfect balance for yourself. Ultimately, you must be honest with yourself.

Life will include some predictable transition periods. You can expect change. You may also feel excessive stress during these transition points. Integrity to your values and resolute control in each of life's sectors will make these periods much easier. Accept each and attempt to grow in each.

Finally, there is an inextricable connection between each area of life. As we seek wholeness, we come to understand the deep influence one role has on another. Continuing in a boring occupation, one with no hope of advancement, will affect your marriage, will affect your financial outlook, and will affect your health if this acceptance of the status quo is allowed to persist. Similarly, the refusal to consider your personal health by not getting enough sleep and proper nutrition will have an effect on your job performance and will negatively affect your emotional and mental faculties. That's the downside of connection. The positive aspect is that growth in any one area of life will positively affect other facets, too. Enrichment in one dimension will produce enrichment in another. In fact, growth in one dimension will, in reality, produce growth in all other dimensions.

Understanding this principle provides life planners with many more options. When you observe a deficiency in one life sector, you can resolve it in several different ways. You not only have the option of working directly with that dimension, but you also have the possibility of working in another dimension with the expectation that growth in that dimension will produce enrichment in the deficient facet. For example, career counselors frequently advise those seeking advancement to first consider their health, knowing that the improvement in energy level gained from proper diet and exercise will have a tremendous effect on the stamina required for superior sales ability or superior time management in business. This will, in turn, affect the prospect for long-term affluence which, in turn, has an undeniable effect on quality of married life given the fact that studies show finances are the most often mentioned topic of quarreling among spouses. The lesson is clear. An incremental change in one dimension has an effect on the whole.

The Wheel of Life Balance

A wheel represents the wholeness of life. Some refer to it as the "wheel of life" with spokes coming from the center. The axle, or center, is our true self. This self includes our individuality, our abilities, and our potential. From this self extend spokes that we have identified as the eight dimensions of life. To the extent that all spokes are present, and all spokes are developed, you have a strong wheel, one that can turn and glide with minimal resistance through life.

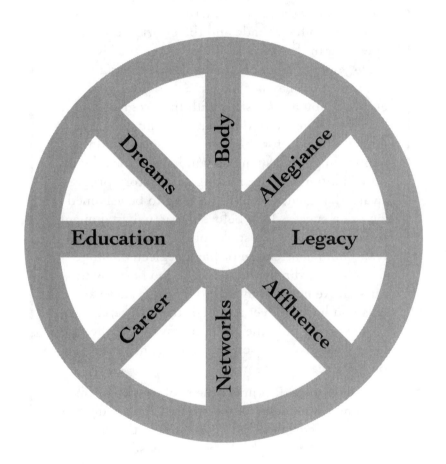

The Wheel of Life

Activity

Complete a short simple exercise that will visually help gauge the balance in your life. Take each of the eight spokes, one at a time, and assess your level of progress in that area. Consider both the progress you would like to have made and the effort you are expending in that facet of life to gauge the level. Grade yourself from one to eight, eight being your optimum. You may not have reached your goal as yet, but if you are satisfied with the progress and the effort you have exerted in that area thus far, give yourself an eight for this role. As discussed in the chapter on goals, as long as you have resolved what you will attain and are making satisfactory progress toward that goal, you have nothing to be ashamed of. You are a success long before the actual attainment. However, if there is a spoke of life which you have given minimal attention or have neglected, gauge yourself accordingly, but don't be too harsh with yourself. Remember, in each dimension these are goals you have not yet attained. In this exercise you are measuring only the attention given and the rate of personal progress you are making, not whether you have reached the goal.

Once finished, connect the spokes with a rim from one to the next. Visually, you can actually see where your wheel is "flat." Remember, the more uniformly round your wheel, the more easily it rolls over the terrain. Are there any spokes on your wheel that are especially short? Can you see where perhaps some of the roughness of your ride through life might be attributed to the condition of your wheel rather than to the terrain you have traveled? Resolve now to work in those areas where renewal is needed.

Before leaving this activity, be certain you have written measurable goals that provide you with a picture of what you wish to attain in each life sector. This is added assurance that you will not neglect any role. Work on each spoke beginning with one in which you feel especially deficient. Once you have made progress working on each life dimension and have begun repairing the "broken spokes," watch your self-esteem soar! You can anticipate a smoother, more fulfilling ride in your life journey!

Time Balance

Life balance also requires a balance of time. For those neglected areas, it may be necessary to schedule time to expand your horizons. Balance, of course, does not mean equal time for each category of interest. Most of us will spend far more time at work or at home with children than cultivating friendships or in concentrated time working on mental or emotional growth. Balance in time allocation means allocating adequate time to promote personal growth. A conscious effort to be well-rounded prevents us from using too much energy in one life category to the detriment of the others.

Aristotle, the Greek philosopher, took a concept from geometry, *the golden mean*, and speculated about its application in personal life. He came to the conclusion that extremes in any pursuit of life are detrimental to personal growth. We all know the stereotype of the successful business executive who is so busy with his career that he neglects family and friends, denying himself and his loved ones the quality of life his business was meant to support. It is a worthwhile habit when planning for the week to schedule time for each role.

Polar Balance

This idea of the golden mean reminds us that throughout history philosophers have called our attention to the need for balance in all activities. In the Orient, the apparent opposing forces are called Yin and Yang. As the physical world is filled with opposites (positive and negative poles on a magnet, positive and negative electrical currents, hot and cold), so mentally we must deal with these opposites. For example, we all know that excess work without time for relaxation is detrimental to emotional well-being; however, where is the perfect balance? At what point can I say a colleague in business is working too many hours and not allotting enough time for renewal? Each of us has to resolve these issues for ourselves. The way to resolution is through prayer, meditation, trial and error, and experience in living. As the environment around us changes, so the solution to the delicate balance shifts.

Periodically review your personal balance in such areas as:

♦ Balance between being busy with projects and taking time for reflection, to review where you are going and how you'll get there.

♦ Balance between a focus on your needs and others' needs; we all know some people who become martyrs to the needs of others, and other people whose attention is solely focused on their own comforts.

♦ Balance between seeking perfection in your creative projects versus the acceptance of imperfection. You can be stifled if you insist you cannot move on until near-perfection is achieved; however, accepting mediocrity destroys the fulfillment which comes with excellence.

♦ Balance between sensitivity to principle versus sensitivity to people. Principles are vital, but if you inflexibly stick to the rules without considering others' needs, no one is served.

♦ Balance between a concern for physical and real needs and concern for abstract (philosophical) and spiritual aspects of life

A balanced person is one who is continually seeking the perfect but ever-changing equilibrium between these opposite poles in life. Both poles have their place. People can be so concerned with sharing every available moment with their children that they neglect career planning. They bounce from one job to another, unintentionally providing an unstable environment for their beloved children. On the other hand, workaholics are so busy providing security for themselves and their children that they have little time for their family's emotional security. Reflection and meditation will help you to evaluate your own course, as you keep in mind that the perfect balance will always be elusive.

One other major aspect of balance concerns goals, those that benefit you only as opposed to the fulfillment of goals that will enrich others and society in general. To be excited about life and inspire others, you'll need goals that give something back to humanity.

> **TRANSFORMATION:**
>
> *Be considerate of the polar opposites in life, seeking to strike an ever-changing delicate balance between them.*
>
> "And the God of all grace, who called you to his eternal glory in Christ, after you have suffered a little while, will Himself restore you and make you strong, firm and steadfast."
> (1 Peter 5:10)

This is especially true in the later years of life. There comes a point when a veteran salesman's new goal of ten percent more sales over last year's sales, which were ten percent over the previous year's, and 20 percent over the year before that, fails to stimulate. The subtle shift to including goals that simultaneously benefit others is needed. Those who have made this shift say that when they invented personal goals, they could only excite themselves. Once they sought the fulfillment of goals outside themselves they began to attract and inspire others, too. Some describe this phenomenon as attracting *universal forces* that gave them power for action far beyond what they had experienced in the past. Such opportunities for growth are possible if we are sensitive to these delicate balances in life.

Summary

There are two types of balance. There is the balance that comes from seeking goal-fulfillment in all eight life sections, not concentrating efforts on one life dimension to the detriment of others. Then there is the delicate balance between the various poles of life, coming to grips with the age-old philosophical questions and finding answers that are practical and practicable for you. These two aspects will occupy you the rest of your life, since your environment and circumstances continually change. Though you'll never attain the perfect balance (life isn't stagnant), the continuous search, not the attainment, will assure you of continual fulfillment.

"[Imagination] reveals itself in the balance or reconciliation of opposite or discordant qualities: of sameness, with difference; of general, with the concrete; the idea, with the image; the individual, with the representative; the sense of novelty and freshness, with old and familiar objects; a more than usual state of emotion, with more than usual order; judgment ever awake and steady self-possession, with enthusiasm and feeling profound or vehement; and while it blends and harmonizes the natural and the artificial, still subordinates art to nature; the manner to the matter; and our admiration of poet to our sympathy with the poetry." (Samuel Taylor Coleridge)

"For God did not give us a spirit of timidity, but a spirit of power, of love and of self-discipline." (2 Timothy 1:7)

CHAPTER 13

A New Beginning

One of my favorite quotations which has helped me through a number of difficulties is Psalm 37:25: "I was young and now I am old, yet I have never seen the righteous forsaken or their children begging bread." I have always been comforted from the optimism inherent in that verse. When I wasn't sure what would happen or was worried about the future, I was certain that if I did what I could under the circumstances, things would work out favorably. When one of my daughters was in her middle teens, I was worried about her association and her future. No amount of reasoning with her seemed to help. I turned to this verse and was renewed in the belief that if I continued to do what I could, and all I could do in this case was to continue to show love, somehow things would work out. Sure enough, they did! At other times when faced with perplexing decisions, I've asked, "Is this decision fair? Am I hurting anyone? Do I believe it is in the best interest of all concerned?" I knew if I could answer "Yes," I couldn't be too far off the results I wanted. As you know, at times, the most difficult part of any ordeal is the agony of not knowing what will happen and just having to wait. We can usually muddle through any adversity but it's the worry and anxiety in the meantime that's so disquieting. The optimism in that verse in Psalms has never disappointed me.

Also, the traditional values, the biblical values, the values you were probably taught when young, and that you intuitively feel are credible, these values have proven to be trustworthy. Current research continually confirms what you already know deep down within you. I have just attempted to put this knowledge in perspective and in a practical, usable form for you and to remind you, if you are a Christian, you are not asked to defer your happiness to some future date. Jesus said, "Ask and you will receive, and your joy will be complete." (John 16:24) A frequent refrain in Scripture is the exhortation to rejoice, to be glad, and to be happy.

This optimistic perspective is what I have stressed to you. A full life means, not that you have experienced a great quantity of adventures, but that you have experienced in good measure the rewards found in each of eight life dimensions. Unfortunately, unless you consciously contemplate your standing in each of these sectors, your life can be left to chance. Your life is too precious to be left to chance, and that's what you're doing if you act without a definite plan. I hope you truly believe this by now.

I hope you also see the necessity for growth. Life is growth. Without growth and regeneration of new cells, any physical organism is doomed to certain death. The same fate is true of life. If you fail to grow mentally, emotionally, or spiritually, your life dries up.

Life is an infinite journey with no finish line in sight. The prospect is for continual growth, reflection, and improvement. You are going to be with yourself for a long time. You might as well like yourself. You might as well enjoy your own company. You can do that by working to be the kind of person you would like for your own friend. You can grow to become that ideal person. You'll never get bored with the project! The further along you are in your journey and the further you progress, the clearer the picture you have of who you are and who you really want to be. I sincerely expect that the more time you spend with yourself, the closer your friendship toward yourself will become and the closer you will come to attaining your ideal self. As a result, you will respect and esteem yourself more, and so will others!

The Dichotomy

I never cease to be amazed at the dichotomy. It's so simple, and yet it appears so difficult. A fulfilled life is very simple. It's as simple as being balanced in the different aspects of your life, making room for growth and renewal in each. It's just saying, "I know I need this in my life, and I am going to find the means during my journey to attain what I know I need." By contemplating what is needed, you'll find within yourself those answers. Through the miracle of life, each organism knows inherently, intuitively, what it needs to prosper, to experience a sense of well-being. It's that simple, periodical assessment of your life and what you need, then resolving to find it.

The complex side of the dichotomy is that there are infinite possibilities and infinite variables. If seen from that vantage, life is difficult. "With so many possibilities, how can I possibly pick the right one for me? I don't have the experience. I don't have the background or the ability," you may tell yourself. Stop! Don't tell yourself some thing that is not true, or you'll delude yourself into believing it. Inherent in all organisms are the necessities for survival and prosperity. Within you are the secrets for growth and life satisfaction. Experience and ability are not the determinants, desire is. Fulfilling your desire does not mean idle dreaming, but firmly deciding what you want and resolving to get it.

Somerset Maugham wrote a short story about a man who loses his long-held job as a janitor in a church because he can't read. Dejected and on his way home after being dismissed, he has an urge for a cigarette. Much to his disappointment, he realizes he hasn't any and that there are no stores in the area that sell them. "There should be a store around here, it's needed," he thinks. That thought leads him to the next one,

> **TRANSFORMATION:**
>
> *Well-being comes not from avoiding pain and problems but from successfully confronting them.*
>
> "Consider it pure joy, my brothers, whenever you face trials of many kinds, because you know that the testing of your faith develops perserverance." (James 1:2,3)

"Wouldn't it be nice if I opened such a shop?" So that's what he does. In fact, he opens many such stores by asking, "Where else is a store like this needed?" Years later, when his banker asks him to sign a document, the man admits, "I can't read that." The banker is shocked. "I can't believe that you're a rich and successful man. Just imagine where you'd be now if you could read!" The man stops and thinks for a moment and says, "I know exactly where I'd be if I could read. I'd still be the janitor at the church!" In his case, inability was not a hindrance but a help. This is true for all of us. Ability and circumstances are not the deciding factors—a firm decision to do our best is!

Fulfillment Predictors

One of the lessons of this story is borne out by research. Fulfillment does not come from avoiding problems, but just the opposite. Often pain and difficulty have a way of leading to happiness if you just bear up under the pain until it passes. This is a seeming anomaly of nature. The opposite seems true. As a result, most people look for happiness by trying to avoid pain and suffering. They are doing the opposite of what may bring them happiness. Fulfillment comes from living, attempting, trying, not from avoiding. Fulfillment is a product of action.

Though fulfillment is among the most sought-after rewards in life, it is widely misunderstood. People seek fulfillment, but it can't be found by seeking. This was well demonstrated by the experience of one of the most astute historians and thinkers of our time, the late Will Durant. He once confided in his writing that he had sought happiness first in knowledge, then in travel, in wealth and in his writing but found disillusionment and fatigue. One day he observed a woman waiting at a train station with a sleeping child in her arms. A man approached from an arriving train and came over and tenderly kissed the woman and child. They then drove off together in noticeable bliss. Durant concluded that, "Every normal function of life holds some delight."

Fulfillment is not found by seeking it—it's found by living. It's not a goal to seek but a by-product of living successfully. Successful living is the result of living a balanced life, making room for all the ingredients, experiencing in measure all its diverse facets. As stated by another renowned thinker, Erick Fromm, "Happiness is proof of partial or total success in the art of living."

Sometimes we forget that fulfillment is not a destination, it's the path we choose to take. Let's say you plan to go to a particular place in a nearby city. There are many possible routes to choose to get there. You could take local two-lane roads, or you could choose an expressway. Local roads could mean stop-and-go traffic and long waits at traffic lights. Taking the expressway at the right time of day could avoid the hassle and may make the difference

> **TRANSFORMATION:**
>
> *Fulfillment cannot be found by seeking—it's a by-product of living successfully.*
>
> "The Lord Jesus himself said, 'It is more blessed to give than to receive.' " (Acts 20:35)

between getting to your destination stress-free. The same is true with journeys in life. You choose how you want to get where you want to go. You decide which roads you will take. Will you take the advice of others who have taken the trip before? Will you take a route relatively free of congestion, or will you choose the way filled with aggravation and needless detours? You'll be as fulfilled as you make up your mind to be.

Over the years I have kept track of surveys on fulfillment and happiness. They all confirm the same discovery. Fulfillment does not correlate with age, sex, or income level. There are certain predictors of fulfillment, though. A stable marriage is one. Unmarried people are shown by surveys to be generally less happy than those who are. A strong faith in a higher power is another indicator. In fact, people with strong faith are twice as likely to be happy than those with little faith. Having a satisfying job is also a major predictor of fulfillment. Only love and marriage have been found to be greater predictors.

What do these data tell us? The traditional values, the biblical values, have stood the test of time. They are worthy of being followed. Also, fulfillment comes from making room for all eight life dimensions. Fulfillment is the result of a balanced existence. Frequently, upon resolving to open their lives to all these important realms, people report a measure of immediate fulfillment. External situations will have little to do with it, but there are major correlates to well-being. The following principles come from various research studies and surveys I've collected or personally done over the years.

If you are to have well-being and fulfillment, don't seek external position or situation but seek first:

♦ *To develop the self-esteem that comes from liking yourself.* Live and experience a life that will allow you to feel good about yourself. Start by building on any limited success you can point to from past experience. There will always be something to remind you that you have done some things right. Build from there.

♦ *To live in the present.* Focus on the moment without dwelling on the past or future. You can change the present immediately and as a result, feel a strong sense of control in your life. Not feeling in control creates bitterness and frustration.

♦ *To be optimistic.* Think in terms of positive outcomes rather than negative. You have already learned that optimism begets optimism. You'll always go in the direction you are pointed. Point yourself toward positive outcomes, and it's difficult to reach the negative.

♦ *To build your faith.* Faith is related to optimism, but it adds the spiritual dimension. Faith reminds you that you don't have to do it all by yourself. There are higher powers working in the universe that can help you bring about a mutual good.

♦ *To be caring.* Taking attention off yourself and focusing on the benefits to others leads to their well-being and leaves you with a sense of satisfaction that cannot be gained any other way. Try to experience this feeling more often.

♦ *To remember that fulfillment is not found at the end of the road but is the journey itself.* Keep busy. Fulfillment and happiness are linked to seeing worthwhile changes resulting from your efforts. Don't look for fulfillment only at the end of the project; be receptive to it as you progress in the right direction.

Focus not on the outcome, not suspending feeling until you attain a good end, but focus on the here and now. "What can I do today that will be working toward the eventual fulfillment of my goals?" Each day is a link in the chain of life. Each day can provide some positive outcomes that can be added as another link in your life. Even if you only learn today what not to do next time, that is still beneficial knowledge.

Misconceptions

In each chapter, I have called attention to one or two major misconceptions that people have embraced as self-evident but in reality are far from accurate. To be fulfilled, major shifts in perception, action, and effort are required, which explains why so few people distinguish themselves from the majority. Probably the most pervasive misconception is the idea that pain is to be feared. If you are to distinguish yourself, you must train yourself to avoid using the momentary reflex of pain avoidance. Pain, both mental and physical, and the discomfort that comes from change are not to be feared. Do not avoid adversity, but embrace it, for without adversity you would have no way of distinguishing yourself. A reason the vast majority never rise above the mediocre is that as they come upon an illusionary barrier, they don't test it. The first time they encounter adversity, when they embark upon a new idea or project, the majority use this adversity as an excuse to abandon the course.

As a successful person, you will train yourself to react just the opposite. An adversity encountered is the first opportunity you have to leave the vast majority behind you. Were it not for the adversity, most anyone would be doing what you wish to do. People are hindered by the prospect of pain, pain being experienced as physical adversity, mental tension, emotional anxiety, or depression. However, as the athlete trains himself to endure pain and recognizes it as a sign that his muscles are being taxed beyond their previous limit and therefore being strengthened, so the athlete in living recognizes that pain almost always leads to the strengthening of his abilities and resolve. Welcome pain and fear as an indication of an opportunity to grow.

The other paradigm shift, or transformation, worthy of embracing is to build upon your present situation. Start where you are now. Build from your present non-threatening circumstances. Resist the tendency to believe success will come only with a complete revision of your life, with some completely new endeavor. That's a misconception. The saying goes, "The grass is always greener..." Success can be built on any and every circumstance. Proof of this is that fulfillment and happiness are right now being experienced by people in circumstances similar to yours.

> **TRANSFORMATION:**
>
> *Enduring pain and adversity is what will set you apart from others; welcome the opportunity.*
>
> "And the God of all grace, who called you to his eternal glory in Christ, after you have suffered a little while, will himself restore you and make you strong, firm and steadfast." (1 Peter 5:10)

So avoid the mistaken reasoning that says if you are not happy or fulfilled right now, you must start all over in some completely new direction. First explore the options available in your present circumstances before acting on the knee-jerk reaction that you must start completely anew. In your present situation you've learned what doesn't work, so you're that much farther along. You need only look for what will work now that you've eliminated what doesn't.

Bill started out as a jeweler. Though he had exceptional ability, after several years he felt he just couldn't make enough money doing repairs and making custom pieces. "There is just too much competition," he said. He decided what he really wanted, what would really make him happy, was to open an art gallery. He pooled his savings and opened the store. It didn't take long for him to admit retail sales had its own set of difficulties. After struggling for years, he heeded the beckoning of a friend who persuaded him to work with him in the movie industry as a production assistant. Unfortunately, that did not bring him the success and happiness he sought.

During all these many years, he had continued to do custom jewelry work for friends and referrals, which he treated as a hobby. One day he realized he was actually making more money on these side jobs than on his professed occupations that changed frequently. Once he admitted each occupation had its own set of drawbacks, he was ready to settle down to his original occupation—custom jewelry design and consulting. Recognizing what his abilities and interests really were, he began to feel for the first time a sense of success and satisfaction. It had taken him many years, and he had come full circle, but he finally experienced the contentment he had so voraciously sought. Unfortunately many don't come to this realization until late in life, and some never see it—that fulfillment is not in the future and that contentment can usually be experienced wherever you are in life. Don't take twenty or thirty years, as it took Bill, to experience what you can almost immediately experience if you make up your mind to do so.

Activity

This exercise may help you bring together some of these ideas. It will help you to know yourself better. Many of us go through the motions of living and never really stop to ask, "What do I really like to do? What brings me true enjoyment?" Similarly, many of us never really think about who we are and how we are unique. This exercise should help you find some of these insights.

This may take you fifteen minutes or so; it's the most powerful exercise I know to help you gain perspective and focus on directions. I suggest you ask yourself these rather simple questions and then write down the answers:

♦ How would I describe myself to myself if I had to choose no more than five words or phrases?

♦ If I were looking back on my life, how would I like others to describe me? (Use no more than five adjectives or phrases.)

♦ If I could find the time, what several things (list at least three or four) would I like to spend more time doing?

♦ If I could easily accomplish them without serious consequences, what several things would I change or eliminate in my life or about my life?

Once you ask and answer these simple questions, I guarantee you will learn some things about yourself that you did not know before. You will know with little doubt what is of value to you. You will have a clearer picture of who you are and how to be that person. This exercise will also provide you with the direction you need to reorder your life in such a way that you use your time most meaningfully.

Armed with these insights, next go about devising how you can incorporate those activities you desire more of in your life.

How might you eliminate or change the life aspects that most irritate you? It stands to reason if you can do more of the things you enjoy and put yourself in less of the situations you hate, life will become more fulfilling.

In general, people, as they get older, look back and say things such as, "I wish I had spent more time with my family," "I wish I had pursued a job I enjoyed," "I wish I had spent more time with my friends," "I wish I had taken more chances," "I wish I hadn't been so worried about what others thought or would say about me."

Whatever you wrote in response to the above exercise, take the time now to firm up your list. Use it daily when you plan your coming day as a reminder of what you have decided to change about yourself. Acting, doing things, making changes impresses upon you that you are not shackled with a depressing life. You have a right to decide what you want to do with your time. Once you realize you have control over your destiny, you really begin to live. You *do* have mastery over your future.

Now do one last thing as part of the exercise. Carry the lists with you for a few days, especially the list of things you don't like doing. By allowing your subconscious mind to incubate, you will come to some exciting, helpful insights about yourself. Try it, you are in for some surprises! Then follow through, making the changes you need to make.

For example, if you find certain assignments at work are boring or generally uninteresting, you have learned a valuable piece of information. Take a few days, let your subconscious mind work on it, helping you to find a solution. You will usually stumble on some simple options. Transferring to a different department, delegating the job to someone else, volunteering for a more difficult task, but one you would enjoy more, are all options. Simply let your mind work on that task and, once resolved, pick the next item on your list of things you want to change or improve and repeat the procedure.

Two Fulfillment Principles

This idea of fulfillment is a critical discovery. I find a great many people who are busy and successful on the surface don't really enjoy themselves at heart. For these people, it is imperative that they realize how many things they are doing by rote but not really enjoying. I suggest two principles that will lead to broader and deeper contentment in life:

(1) Wake up and learn to enjoy life's process, not just the end results.

The affirmation is repeated in Scripture, "My soul rejoices in my God!" (Isaiah 61:10) Pause to experience and savor what is happening at the moment. Be aware of what is happening around you. Recognize the human mechanism was conceived to allow us to do many things at one time without consciously being aware of them. This mechanism is necessary for efficiency. I can be driving my car down the road, listening to the radio, eating an apple, and carrying on a conversation simultaneously. That's efficiency, but am I really experiencing the moment? Probably not. That is where awareness must be inserted into the setting. This is just another example of one of the dichotomies of life—efficiency of actions versus experiencing of the moment. Both have their place. But you might try to spend a little extra time experiencing the moment.

(2) Look for havens of relaxation, opportunities, or rituals—or even places that allow you a change of pace.

A health club, a quiet restaurant, or even a favorite park bench where you can relax and rejuvenate will fill the bill. An excellent way to eliminate the clutter in life is to regularly take the time to be alone. The formal process is known as meditation, but the practice need not be formal at all. Just setting aside the time to be alone, to reflect, to seek direction, or simply to rejuvenate is informal meditation. I've noted that some are rather apprehensive and suspicious of the term *meditation* which might give a connotation of an extreme mystical exercise. Call it meditation, contemplation, prayer, or listening to God.

The Italian psychologist, Assogioli, in the early part of this century wrote an insightful discourse on meditation. He suggested three major reasons for meditation: for reflection on one's life course, for reception of intuition, and for creativity. These all can have practical applications in life now. However, for any type of contemplation, prayer, or meditation to benefit you, some key elements are required:

♦ Physical relaxation to eliminate all muscle and nervous tension

♦ Emotional tranquillity

♦ Mental resolution to direct inward rather than outward

There are many ways to eliminate the mind's clutter allowing for relaxation and the ability to enjoy being alone. You may want to get a book that provides practical instruction on methods of prayer and meditation that will work for you. To be able to solve problems or to be aware of life passing by you, you must be able to eliminate needless distraction and focus on a particular problem at hand. Be receptive to the physical sensations you are feeling at the moment. Learn to enjoy your own company.

My wife's art studio is, at times, so cluttered with materials, equipment, half-finished projects, and paraphernalia that she feels discouraged just walking into the room. During these occasional times, she lacks the motivation to work on a project, since it means first wading through the obstacles to even begin to do anything creative. This is true on a much larger scale. Life can be so cluttered with half-finished projects and experiences that any person with creative drive might not know where to begin. Regular periods of meditation help to keep things in order, help to sort through the clutter. Regular moments of silence make it clear what is most important in your life and which actions are imperative under the present circumstance.

Happy Endings

Everyone likes to see a happy ending. The most popular novels and movies invariably portray a final resolution of the conflict. There is something satisfying about a happy ending to a story, and guess what? I firmly believe we can all have happy endings. In your life, *you* are the author! As author, you can write and then rewrite the ending if you are dissatisfied with the first draft. You can crumble up and throw away the first draft, your first attempt, just as a writer may crumble up her paper, throw it out, and start over.

Consider this: When you think about it, every set of events does have a happy ending if allowed to play itself out. The problem is, many lack the patience to stay for the happy ending. They figuratively either put down the book or walk out of the theater without waiting to see the final outcome. I challenge you to think of any event in history that has not had a satisfying ending to it. The important point to remember is every event has consequences far beyond their immediate presence. Think of some of the worst disasters in history. For example, consider the six million Jews who died in concentration camps during World War II. It's difficult to imagine a drama with a more horrifying and negative ending. However, was that really the end of the story? Did those victims die in vain? Of course not. Were there no consequences from those events? Their sufferings have inspired millions to appreciate freedom and to work to assure that a similar tragedy will never occur again. Those events also provided the inspiration and justification for the creation of a national homeland for those of Jewish origin and have provided Jews with more reasons to be proud of their heritage.

I could go on citing evidence to prove that this tragedy in history had a negative ending only if we isolate the heinous events without waiting for ultimate resolutions. This story is yet unfinished some fifty years later. I trust that for centuries this event will serve as an inspiration and a warning to future generations. There are always some aspects of an event that can be considered happy endings even now in this physical world, even without granting the existence of an afterlife (which, according to surveys, is a real possibility to most Americans and an absolute to any Christian).

I don't mean to be simplistic. I only wish to submit that every event in the past can be analyzed and interpreted from positive perspectives. These aren't the only valid interpretations, but there are always positive outcomes to consider. *You can choose which interpretation you wish to accept!*

A drunk driver kills a child; drug addiction lures a teenager to a life of crime; parents are killed in a car accident—these are tragic events, but they are not the end. Good and positive results can spring and have sprung from similar heartbreaking experiences. We have to look for the long-term outcome.

I know the phrase "it's never too late" is trite and over-used, but it definitely applies in life. It is never too late to transform your life to result in a happy ending. A person living a selfish, thoughtless existence throughout his life can leave a positive legacy with a heartfelt and sincere apology to those he hurt. Such a transformation from negative to positive could take place in his final moments. Even at the point of his death, with no one around, a sincere prayer of regret and sorrow coupled with a request that somehow the misery he inflicted on others could be rectified could very well galvanize the universal forces to produce that good result. The end result can be positive. So, from wherever you begin your life journey or however it may appear at the moment, it is never too late to begin again.

I wish you well. I know you can accomplish your dreams. Remember that, though your task may be formidable, there will always be others, even unknown to you, that share your determination and faith in your personal happy ending.

The Beginning

The one truth that runs throughout this book is that you can make your life what you wish it to be now. There is no reason to put up with circumstances that annoy or frustrate you without attempting to change them. There is no reason to be bullied by events and people. There is no reason to accept adversity as

> **TRANSFORMATION:**
>
> *All events can have happy endings if we observe them from a long-term standpoint.*
>
> "Consider it pure joy, my brothers, whenever you face trials of many kinds, because you know that the testing of your faith develops perseverance. Perseverance must finish its work so that you may be mature and complete, not lacking anything." (James 1:2-4)

defeat in any undertaking. Remember Jesus' promise, "Ask and you will receive and your joy will be complete." (John 16:24) You can do *something* about any set of circumstances. When you are beset with problems and you are perplexed with what your ultimate course of action should be, here, too, at least something can be done. Some small step can be taken to affirm to yourself and to the world outside yourself that you intend to change what is presently a reality. You will not accept events as they are without a fight. Scripture says of a godly man, "How great is his joy in the victories you give!" (Psalm 21:1) Your ability to affirm to yourself that events can and will change is one of your greatest assets. You affirm this by thought, but more importantly by doing something. If nothing else, you can meditate on your next step and resolve in your mind that somehow you will make changes.

> **TRANSFORMATION:**
>
> *You are writing the story of your life at this moment.*
>
> "Continue to work out your salvation with fear and trembling." (Philippians 2:12)

Please take away this one final assurance with you. You have all you need! You've been endowed with a miraculous mind and body. The powers of intuition and creativity designed within you will serve you through problem and opportunity. If you are a believer in the power of God, you may ask for and receive His guidance and security. If you are a Christian, you can recall times when you have experienced such assistance that can be explained only as being divine in origin. Finally, you have the wisdom of the Bible from which I've offered practical application. In the Preface, I mentioned the special promise found in Psalms. I close by quoting it again. Living by these divine principles, you can be spared unnecessary suffering and difficulties and be assured of unsurpassed direction:

The law of the LORD is perfect, reviving the soul.

The statutes of the LORD are trustworthy, making wise the simple.

The precepts of the LORD are right, giving joy to the heart.

The commands of the LORD are radiant, giving light to the eyes.

By them is your servant warned; in keeping them there is great reward.

(Psalm 19:7,8,11)

For what more can you ask? You have all you need for finding fulfillment! So take charge of your life. Don't be pushed around by others' assessments that it's hopeless. Voice a personal protest, whether it be aloud for others to hear or within yourself, that you will not stand for things as they are. To carry with you hope rather than despair is your choice. Picture a happy ending for yourself this year, another for next year, and still another for five years and then ten years from now. Remember, you are writing the story of your life now; you're living the story of your

TRANSFORMATION:

You are writing the story of your life at this moment.

"Continue to work out your salvation with fear and trembling." (Philippians 2:12)

life now. Please make up your mind now that it will include a happy ending!

> "We but half express ourselves, and are ashamed of that divine idea which each of us represents. Nothing can bring you peace but yourself."
> (Ralph Waldo Emerson)

> "Command those...to put their hope in God, who richly provides us with everything for our enjoyment. Command them to do good, to be rich in good deeds, and to be generous, willing to share. In this way they will lay up treasure for themselves as a firm foundation for the coming age, so they may take hold of the life that is truly life."
> (1 Timothy 6:17-19)